THE GENERAL CONVENTION
OF THE EPISCOPAL CHURCH

THE
GENERAL
CONVENTION
OF THE
EPISCOPAL
CHURCH

BOB N. WALLACE
Foreword by Scott Field Bailey

A CROSSROAD BOOK
THE SEABURY PRESS • NEW YORK

The Seabury Press
815 Second Avenue
New York, N.Y. 10017

Copyright © 1976 by The Seabury Press, Inc.

Printed in the United States of America

LIBRARY OF CONGRESS CATALOGING IN PUBLICATION DATA

Wallace, Bob N   1932–
The General Convention of the Episcopal Church.
"A Crossroad book."
1. Protestant Episcopal Church in the U.S.A.
General Convention. I. Title.
BX5820.W34   262.'03   76–10156   ISBN 0–8164–1212–X

This book is dedicated to—

The Rev. John B. Coburn, President of the House of Deputies, for his understanding as a friend and his inspiration as a leader; to—

The Rt. Rev. Scott Field Bailey, Executive Officer of the General Convention, for his guidance and friendship during the transition of General Convention; and to—

Jane, my wife, without whose dedication, knowledge of the Church, and constant supportive love, it could not have been written.

ACKNOWLEDGMENTS

The author would like to acknowledge the help and assistance of the following persons and offices in the preparation of this book: the Rt. Rev. Scott Field Bailey, Executive Officer of General Convention, whose assistance in reading the original manuscript for accuracy and the proper stating of issues was invaluable; Dr. V. Nelle Bellamy, Archivist of the Episcopal Church; and Elinor S. Hearn, assistant to the Archivist of the Archives and Historical Collection of the Episcopal Church, Austin, Texas, for providing invaluable assistance in preparing the chronological listing of the admission of dioceses as well as the listing of Secretaries of the House of Bishops, Secretaries of the House of Deputies, and Treasurers of the General Convention. Assistance in accuracy has also been given by Mr. James Winning, Mrs. Jane Wallace, Mr. Robert Dye, and Miss Avis Harvey.

The author would also like to acknowledge the assistance gained from the many meetings and conferences held with committees, commissions, and various agencies of the Episcopal Church. The persons he has had the privilege of working with over the past few years have given great insight into the mind and spirit of the Church as it is expressed through the General Convention.

CONTENTS

FOREWORD

The election of delegates to General Convention by a diocese is always a moment of great import to the Church and an occasion of excitement to the elected delegate. Only favored and trusted sons and daughters are chosen by the Church to join with the bishops in making the judgments that determine the doctrine, discipline, and worship of the Episcopal Church. It is in such conciliar action that we look for our Lord's will for his Church.

At the Minnesota Convention in 1976, approximately sixty percent of the membership of the House of Deputies will be newly elected; and twenty percent of the House of Bishops will be composed of new bishops. The new deputies and bishops are quite capable of giving their several dioceses competent representation and making conscientious decisions. They will, however, find these chapters on the General Convention an excellent explanation and guide to the legislative processes, as well as a means of identifying the historical perspective of the Episcopal Church.

There is a chapter on the history of General Convention which shows the growth of the Church through sixty-four previous Conventions. Also included are chapters on the structure, process, and administration of Convention. This guide is necessary homework for both old and new deputies, and for anyone who wants to be well informed on the workings of the Church.

As Manager of the 1973 and 1976 General Conventions, Mr.

Wallace carries the responsibility of preparing the facilities and training the Convention personnel who will enable the Church to meet in Minneapolis for the sixty-fifth Convention. Mr. Wallace has served his Church well in preparing this guide to General Convention.

> Scott Field Bailey
> Bishop Coadjutor of West Texas
> Executive Officer of General Convention

PREFACE

It is strange how books come into being. Authors are inspired in many ways to express their thoughts. My inspiration for this brief treatment of the General Convention came through observation. It has been my distinct privilege to attend, *ex officio,* almost all the planning committee meetings of the various aspects of General Convention over the past few years. There seemed to be great enthusiasm and eagerness for a General Convention that would be efficient and well planned. The problems occurred when all the logistics of planning were in place and the people were inserted into the scene. New deputies, especially those attending their first General Convention, appeared overwhelmed with the size of the Convention and the working of its process. There was also the confusing factor that the actual operation of the General Convention changed in 1973 from a diocese-managed Convention to a national Church function. Trying to get the story known throughout the Episcopal Church often proved difficult. Trying to make the newly elected deputies knowledgeable about their task sometimes proved even more difficult.

From this standpoint then, I believed that an effort of this kind could have merit and make a contribution to the fuller understanding of how General Convention operates today and the ways in which the Church-at-large can be involved in it. This is not to be construed as a definitive work on General Convention, nor as a textbook on the subject. It is written from a layman's viewpoint for persons interested in knowing more about a large and complicated undertaking that occurs every three years in the life of the Church.

There are certain helps for the person desiring to know more about the subject of General Convention. For the most part, footnotes have been avoided because most of the technical data has been obtained from the *Journal* of General Convention. The diagrams have been included in an effort to save the reader time, and in the belief that "one picture is worth a thousand words."

The chronological list of the admission of dioceses into General Convention is, to my knowledge, the first of its kind. This list should show the effort of the Episcopal Church over the almost two hundred years of its existence in America. Spans of time when no expansion took place were followed by periods of great activity. This could not be portrayed by an alphabetical listing of the dioceses. The dates and details have been checked by the Episcopal Church archivist, Dr. Nelle Bellamy of Austin, Texas.

Preparing this book has been a labor of love; love for the Church and its visible means of confronting itself and the world through a sometimes imperfect vehicle. Remembering that the Church is not a perfect instrument for the accomplishment of God's purposes for man in this world, neither is the General Convention a perfect instrument in the hands of the Church for the accomplishment of its tasks. Nevertheless it is the vehicle for such accomplishment, and it will be effective only insofar as we understand it and work within its framework.

This book is written for that purpose, and it is dedicated to a fuller and more complete understanding on the part of those people who desire to know more about their Church and how it works. If after you read this book you have realized this purpose, I will have been fulfilled both as a person and an Episcopalian.

> Bob N. Wallace
> November 21, 1975
> Louisville, Kentucky

THE GENERAL CONVENTION
OF THE EPISCOPAL CHURCH

CHAPTER 1

A BRIEF HISTORY OF
THE GENERAL CONVENTION

The first regular session of The General Convention in 1789 occurred at Philadelphia. A constitution was adopted, canons ratified, and an American Book of Common Prayer published. With these and other actions, the unity of American Episcopalians within the Anglican communion was established. Only thirteen years had elapsed since the signing of the Declaration of Independence of the United States.

It had been a turbulent period. The American Revolution had wrought havoc among the political loyalties of the colonists. The Anglican congregations then in existence had suffered from a lack of both leadership and funds. Many laypersons and clergy endured hardships and deprivation because of the severed allegiance to the British Crown. Persecutions, abuses, property destruction, jail, and even banishment from individual colonies resulted.

Due to the chaos and despair among the various Anglican communions throughout the colonies, the Reverend William White, Rector of Christ Church in Philadelphia, proposed that a national Church be formed to bring unity and order out of the discord that existed among the colonial Anglicans. His idea was to form a free and independent Anglican Church on the same order as the evolving confederation of states being developed by the colonial statesmen. Many of those struggling with the national structure were also Anglican churchmen. As a result, similarity of structure and terms eventually existed between the national governing body and the General Convention of the Episcopal Church. A bicameral legislative body came into being in both organizations. However, the General Convention existed as a single house from 1785 until the first regular session in 1789.

The General Convention of 1785, with the Rev. William White serving as President of the first House of Deputies from September 27 to October 7, presented some problems of unity. Some of the churches throughout the land were not united in their efforts and consequently were not represented at the first Convention. New York, North Carolina, and Georgia were absent, various reasons prohibiting their participation. This in no way prohibited those present in Philadelphia from proceeding with the business at hand—the establishment of an American Anglican Church. This included obtaining permission from English archbishops and bishops, through passage of an act of Parliament, to confer episcopal orders on Americans elected by their several jurisdictions. The first draft of a resolution for the organization and revision of the 1662 English Book of Common Prayer, which would exclude prayers for the King of England, was also begun.

The General Convention of 1786, meeting from June 20 to 26 in Philadelphia and from October 10 to 11 in Wilmington, Delaware, again dealt with Prayer Book revision. But it was not until the revisions made at the Convention that the American Prayer Book, by ommitting some of the proposed changes and including the more traditional usages and materials revered by the Church of England, met most of the objections of the English bishops. The American Book of Common Prayer has undergone two revisions since its inception, and will probably continue to do so as it is the living and viable expression of the Episcopal faith. This however, was only the beginning.

In 1789, the suspicion, mistrust, prejudice, and disunity within the struggling Church was resolved, and the episcopate was intact in America. Because the Church of England could not, at this early stage, consecrate American clergymen to the office of bishop, Samuel Seabury, a Connecticut priest, received consecration in 1784 at the hands of the Episcopal (Anglican) Church in Scotland. By 1787, the English Parliament having passed the necessary act, two more American clergymen, William White of Pennsylvania and Samuel Provoost of New York, were consecrated bishops by the Archbishop of Canterbury and other English bishops. The stage was set for the historical General Convention of 1789.

From the end of July until the middle of October the General Convention met and adopted a Constitution which, as subsequently amended, remains the governing document for the Episcopal Church. Its present contents are:

Preamble
Article I.   Of the General Convention
Article II.   Of Bishops
Article III.   Of Bishops Consecrated for Foreign Lands
Article IV.   Of the Standing Committee
Article V.   Of Admission of New Dioceses
Article VI.   Of Missionary Dioceses
Article VII.   Of Provinces
Article VIII.   Of Requests for Ordination
Article IX.   Of Courts
Article X.   Of the Book of Common Prayer
Article XI.   Of Amendments to the Constitution

That General Convention also enacted a body of Canons, the status of which differs from that of the Constitution. The Constitution may only be amended by the concurrent action of both the House of Bishops and the House of Deputies at two successive General Conventions, while Canon law may be changed, altered, or added to by concurrent action of both Houses at a single General Convention. The Canons are now grouped into five sections, called Titles:

Title I.	Organization and Administration
Title II.	Worship
Title III.	The Ministry
Title IV.	Ecclesiastical Discipline
Title V.	Canonical Legislation

The reader is urged to secure a copy of both these documents and study them for a deeper knowledge and understanding of the government of the Episcopal Church. To understand the Constitution and Canons is to understand "how the Church works." They are included in each *Journal* of General Convention, but are also published separately.

The General Convention of 1789 also provided for the publishing of an American Book of Common Prayer. The first edition of 1789, has subsequently been revised twice—in 1892 and in 1928. Revision of the 1928 Book of Common Prayer has been before the General Convention since 1967, at which time it adopted a plan for Prayer Book Revision. An extensive study could be made of the documents and revision of documents that have occurred in the past. This would give an idea of the history of General Convention. Unfortunately, space limitations prohibit this from being done in the present work. Neither is it the purpose of this work to attempt such a study.

There is one approach, however, to seeing the General Convention in historical perspective—through a chronological listing of the organization of dioceses within the Episcopal Church.

There sometimes appeared a span of several years before new areas of mission and ministry were opened. The new frontier had to be opened by early settlers before the Church began its steady westward movement. Such a list is given in this chapter (pages 5–10), and shows the Episcopal Church as a growing, moving, ever-spreading witness for Christ. True, there were periods of stagnation and times of rapid expansion. But, there was always progress, however slow it might have seemed. The reader should take time to study this list carefully, note the growth of the Church, and savor its rich and abundant heritage.

The Constitution is very specific on the procedure and method whereby dioceses are admitted into the General Convention of the Episcopal Church. This can be done by the formation of a new diocese, by the division of an existing diocese, by the joining together of two or more dioceses or parts of two or more dioceses, or by the establishment of a mission diocese. After the very careful process of establishment has been accomplished to the satisfaction of the General Convention, the new diocese is admitted.

*ORGANIZATION OF DIOCESES OF THE EPISCOPAL CHURCH, chronologically through 1973**

1783 Diocese	Maryland
1783 Diocese	Connecticut
1784 Diocese	Massachusetts
1784 Diocese	Pennsylvania
1785 Diocese	New Jersey
1785 Diocese	New York
1785 Diocese	South Carolina
1785 Diocese	Virginia

*This data has been compiled from the master file of diocesan journals in the Archives and Historical Collections of the Episcopal Church. Where some confusion arose, information was checked in General Convention journals and in diocesan histories.

1786	Delaware; organized as a diocese but no bishop until 1841
1790	Rhode Island; organized as diocese; part of Eastern Diocese 1810–1843; 1843 separated and became Diocese of Rhode Island independent
1790 Diocese	Vermont (part of Eastern Diocese 1810–1832)
1802 Diocese	New Hampshire
1810–1843	Eastern Diocese; included Vermont, New Hampshire, Rhode Island, Maine, and Massachusetts
1817 Diocese	North Carolina
1818 Diocese	Ohio
1820 Diocese	Maine
1823 Diocese	Georgia
1826 Diocese	Mississippi
1829 Diocese	Kentucky
1829 Diocese	Tennessee
1830 Diocese	Alabama
1832 Diocese	Michigan
1835 Diocese	Chicago, Illinois; name changed 1884 to Chicago
1835 Diocese	Arkansas; part of a missionary jurisdiction until Primary Convention as diocese in 1871
1838 Diocese	Florida
1838 Diocese	Indianapolis, Indiana; 1903 became Diocese of Indianapolis
1838 Diocese	Louisiana
1838 Diocese	Western New York
1840 Diocese	Missouri
1847	Milwaukee; organized as Diocese of Wisconsin; 1887 name changed to Milwaukee
1849 Diocese	Texas
1850	organized California; 1854 missionary district; 1857 diocese
1850	Liberia; missionary district*
1853 Diocese	Iowa
1853	Oregon; missionary territory of Oregon and Wash-

---

* In 1970 the term "missionary district" was changed to "missionary diocese."

	ington; 1880 missionary district of Oregon; 1889 diocese
1857 Diocese	Minnesota
1859	Colorado; part of missionary jurisdiction of the Northwest; 1865 missionary district of Colorado and parts adjacent; 1887 diocese
1859 Diocese	Kansas
1865 Diocese	Pittsburgh
1866	Utah; missionary territory of Montana, Idaho, and Utah; 1880 Utah and Idaho mission; 1886 Nevada and Utah mission; 1899 missionary district of Salt Lake; 1908 missionary district of Utah; 1972 diocese
1868 Diocese	Albany
1868 Diocese	Central New York
1868 Diocese	Easton
1868 Diocese	Long Island
1868 Diocese	Nebraska
1869	Mexico (independent church); 1904 missionary district; 1922 divided into 3 dioceses*
1871	Bethlehem; Diocese of Central Pennsylvania; 1910 name changed to Diocese of Bethlehem
1871	South Dakota; part of Niobrara Mission; 1884 missionary district of South Dakota; 1971 diocese
1874	Montana; missionary district of Montana, Idaho, and Utah; 1880 missionary district of Montana; 1904 diocese
1874	Haiti; missionary district*
1874	Newark; Diocese of Northern New Jersey; 1886 renamed Diocese of Newark
1874 Diocese	Western Michigan
1875	Dallas; constituted as missionary district of Northern Texas; 1895 Diocese of Dallas
1875 Diocese	Fond du Lac
1875	Northern California; Northern California mission; 1899 missionary district of Sacramento; 1911 Diocese of Sacramento; 1961 name changed to Diocese of Northern California

1875 Diocese	Southern Ohio
1875	West Texas; missionary district of Western Texas; 1904 Diocese of West Texas
1877 Diocese	Quincy
1877 Diocese	Springfield
1877 Diocese	West Virginia
1880	Arizona; missionary jurisdiction; 1893 missionary district; 1959 Diocese
1880	Rio Grande; New Mexico and Arizona missionary jurisdiction; 1892 missionary district of New Mexico and "Texas Areas"; 1927 Diocese of New Mexico and Southwest Texas; 1973 changed name to Diocese of Rio Grande
1881	Olympia; missionary jurisdiction of Washington; 1892 changed name to Olympia; 1911 diocese
1883 Diocese	East Carolina
1884	North Dakota missionary district; 1971 diocese
1884	Wyoming missionary jurisdiction of Wyoming; 1889 missionary jurisdiction of Wyoming and Idaho; 1895 missionary district of Wyoming; 1899 missionary district of Platte and Laramie; 1908 missionary district of Wyoming; 1968 diocese
1889	Western Nebraska; missionary district of the Platte; 1899 missionary jurisdiction of Platte and Laramie; 1900 missionary district of Laramie; 1908 missionary district of Kearney; 1914 missionary district of Western Nebraska; 1946 reunited with Nebraska
1890 Diocese	West Missouri; 1905–1913 called Diocese of Kansas City; 1913 returned to Diocese of West Missouri
1892	Alaska; constituted; 1963 missionary district; 1972 Diocese
1892 Diocese	Southern Virginia
1892	Western Colorado; missionary district of Western Colorado; 1904–1907 a part of Salt Lake mis-

	sionary district; 1907 missionary district of Western Colorado; 1919 reunited with Diocese of Colorado
1893	Northern Michigan; Diocese of Northern Michigan; 1895 renamed Diocese of Marquette; 1937 renamed Diocese of Northern Michigan
1893	South Florida; missionary jurisdiction of Southern Florida; 1923 Diocese of South Florida; 1969 divided into dioceses of Central Florida, Southeast Florida, and Southwest Florida
1893	Spokane; missionary district; 1965 Diocese
1895	Duluth; constituted; 1908 diocese; 1944 reunited with Diocese of Minnesota
1895 Diocese	Lexington
1895 Diocese	Los Angeles
1895	Oklahoma; Oklahoma mission; 1911 missionary district of Eastern Oklahoma was set apart; 1919 two districts reunited; 1937 diocese
1895 Diocese	Washington
1895	Western North Carolina; missionary district of Ashville; 1922 Diocese of Western North Carolina
1896	Idaho; missionary jurisdiction; 1899 missionary jurisdiction of Boise; 1908 missionary jurisdiction of Idaho; 1915 missionary district; 1968 diocese
1899	Northern Indiana; Diocese of Michigan City; 1919 Diocese of Northern Indiana
1901	Philippines missionary district; 1971 divided into 3 dioceses*
1901 Diocese	Western Massachusetts
1901	Puerto Rico missionary district; 1919 Virgin Is. became part of this district*
1902	Hawaii; missionary district of Honolulu; 1961 missionary diocese; 1969 Diocese of Hawaii (name changed)
1903	Western Kansas; missionary district of Salina; 1960

	name changed to missionary district of Western Kansas; 1971 diocese
1904 Diocese	Harrisburg; renamed Central Pennsylvania in 1971
1906	Nevada; missionary district; prior to this Nevada was divided between two other missionary districts; 1971 diocese
1907 Diocese	Atlanta
1908	Eastern Oregon; missionary district; 1971 diocese
1910 Diocese	Erie
1910	Northwest Texas; missionary district of North Texas; 1958 Diocese of Northwest Texas
1911	San Joaquin; missionary district; 1961 diocese
1919	Central America and Panama Canal Zone; missionary district*
1919 Diocese	Southwestern Virginia
1922 Diocese	Upper South Carolina
1929 Diocese	Eau Claire
1931 Diocese	Rochester
1940	Dominican Republic; missionary district*
1947	Virgin Is. became separate missionary district from Puerto Rico*
1956	Central America and Panama Canal Zone separated into two missionary districts*
1960	Taiwan; missionary district*
1963	Columbia; separated from Canal Zone into a missionary district*
1966	Ecuador; missionary district*
1967	Costa Rica, El Salvador, Honduras, Nicaragua, and Guatemala became separate missionary district out of Central America*
1970 Diocese	Central Florida
1970 Diocese	Central Gulf Coast
1973 Diocese	San Diego

In the evolving Episcopal Church's structure, the terms and leadership of the dioceses have changed over the years. Today, the term "diocese" applies to what was formerly known as "missionary dioceses" and to the "Convocation of the American Churches in Europe." In recent years the clergy and bishops of the Church overseas have been native-born persons. This was a conscious effort on the part of the Episcopal Church which resulted in the return to the United States of many American priests and bishops within the last decade.

A brief history of the General Convention would not be complete without a listing of the places the General Convention has met through the years. From its inception, through the division created by the War Between the States, World War I, the Great Depression of the 1930s, World War II, Korea, and Southeast Asia, the Convention has met and addressed itself to the times and to current issues. The reader is encouraged to obtain the historical records of these meetings and learn more about the General Convention of the Episcopal Church from its inception in the United States up to the present.

A TABLE OF THE GENERAL CONVENTIONS

NO.	OPENED CLOSED	PLACE OF MEETING
1	Sept. 27–Oct. 7, 1785	Philadelphia.
2	{ June 20–June 26, 1786 Oct. 10–Oct. 11, 1786	Philadelphia. Wilmington, Del.
3	{ July 28–Aug. 8, 1789 Sept. 29–Oct. 16, 1789	Philadelphia. Philadelphia.
4	Sept. 11–Sept. 19, 1792	New York.
5	Sept. 8–Sept. 18, 1795	Philadelphia.
6	June 11–June 19, 1799	Philadelphia.
7	Sept. 8–Sept. 12, 1801	Trenton, N. J.
8	Sept. 11–Sept. 18, 1804	New York.
9	May 17–May 26, 1808	Baltimore.
10	May 21–May 24, 1811	New Haven.
11	May 17–May 24, 1814	Philadelphia.
12	May 20–May 27, 1817	New York.
13 I	{ May 16–May 24, 1820 Oct. 30–Nov. 3, 1821	Philadelphia. Philadelphia.

NO.	OPENED CLOSED	PLACE OF MEETING
14	May 20–May 26, 1823	Philadelphia.
15	Nov. 7–Nov. 15, 1826	Philadelphia.
16	Aug. 12–Aug. 20, 1829	Philadelphia.
17	Oct. 17–Oct. 31, 1832	New York.
18	Aug. 19–Sept. 1, 1835	Philadelphia.
19	Sept. 5–Sept. 17, 1838	Philadelphia.
20	Oct. 6–Oct. 19, 1841	New York.
21	Oct. 2–Oct. 22, 1844	Philadelphia.
22	Oct. 6–Oct. 28, 1847	New York.
23	Oct. 2–Oct. 16, 1850	Cincinnati.
24	Oct. 5–Oct. 26, 1853	New York.
25	Oct. 1–Oct. 21, 1856	Philadelphia.
26	Oct. 5–Oct. 22, 1859	Richmond, Va.
A1	July 3–July 6, 1861	Montgomery, Ala.
A2	Oct. 16–Oct. 24, 1861	Columbia, S. C.
27	Oct. 1–Oct. 17, 1862	New York.
A3	Nov. 12–Nov. 22, 1862	Augusta, Ga.
28	Oct. 4–Oct. 24, 1865	Philadelphia.
A4	Nov. 8–Nov. 10, 1865	Augusta, Ga.
29	Oct. 7–Oct. 29, 1868	New York.
30	Oct. 4–Oct. 26, 1871	Baltimore.
31	Oct. 7–Nov. 3, 1874	New York.
32	Oct. 3–Oct. 25, 1877	Boston.
33	Oct. 6–Oct. 27, 1880	New York.
34	Oct. 3–Oct. 26, 1883	Philadelphia.
35	Oct. 6–Oct. 28, 1886	Chicago.
36	Oct. 2–Oct. 24, 1889	New York.
37	Oct. 5–Oct. 25, 1892	Baltimore.
38	Oct. 2–Oct. 22, 1895	Minneapolis.
39	Oct. 5–Oct. 25, 1898	Washington.
40	Oct. 2–Oct. 17, 1901	San Francisco.
41	Oct. 5–Oct. 25, 1904	Boston.
42	Oct. 2–Oct. 19, 1907	Richmond, Va.
43	Oct. 5–Oct. 21, 1910	Cincinnati.
44	Oct. 8–Oct. 25, 1913	New York.
45	Oct. 11–Oct. 27, 1916	St. Louis.
46	Oct. 8–Oct. 24, 1919	Detroit.
47	Sept. 6–Sept. 23, 1922	Portland, Oreg.
48	Oct. 7–Oct. 24, 1925	New Orleans, La.
49	Oct. 10–Oct. 25, 1928	Washington, D. C.
50	Sept. 16–Sept. 30, 1931	Denver, Colo.
51	Oct. 10–Oct. 23, 1934	Atlantic City, N. J.

NO.	OPENED CLOSED	PLACE OF MEETING
52	Oct. 6–Oct. 19, 1937	Cincinnati.
53	Oct. 9–Oct. 19, 1940	Kansas City, Mo.
54	Oct. 2–Oct. 11, 1943	Cleveland.
55	Sept. 10–Sept. 20, 1946	Philadelphia.
56	Sept. 26–Oct. 7, 1949	San Francisco.
57	Sept. 8–Sept. 19, 1952	Boston.
58	Sept. 4–Sept. 15, 1955	Honolulu, T. H.
59	Oct. 5–Oct. 17, 1958	Miami Beach, Fla.
60	Sept. 17–Sept. 29, 1961	Detroit, Mich.
61	Oct. 11–Oct. 23, 1964	St. Louis, Mo.
62	Sept. 17–Sept. 27, 1967	Seattle, Wash.
II	Aug. 31–Sept. 5, 1969	South Bend, In.
63	Oct. 11–Oct. 22, 1970	Houston Tx.
64	Sept. 29–Oct. 11, 1973	Louisville Ky.
65	Sept. 11–Sept. 23, 1976	Minneapolis/St. Paul, Mn.

PRESIDING BISHOPS AND PRESIDENTS OF THE HOUSE OF DEPUTIES, 1785–1973

PRESIDING BISHOPS	PRES. HOUSE OF DEPUTIES
1. Bp. William White. 1789	1. Rev. Wm. White, D.D. 1785
2. Bp. Samuel Seabury. 1789	2. Rev. David Griffith. 1786
3. Bp. Samuel Provoost. 1792	3. Rev. Samuel Provoost, D.D. 1786
4. Bp. William White. 1795–1835	4. Bp. Wm. White. 1789
5. Bp. Alexander Viets Griswold. 1838–1841	5. Rev. Wm. Smith, D.D. 1789–1799
6. Bp. Philander Chase. 1844–1850	6. Rev. Abraham Beach, D.D. 1801–1808
Bp. Thomas Church Brownell. 1853–1859	7. Rev. Isaac Wilkins. 1811
7. Bp. Stephen Elliott. 1861	8. Rev. John Croes, D.D. 1814
8. Bp. William Meade. 1861	9. { Rev. Isaac Wilkins, D.D. 1817 / Rev. Wm. H. Wilmer, D.D. 1817
9. Bp. Thomas Church Brownell. 1862	10. Rev. Wm. H. Wilmer, D.D. 1820
10. Bp. Stephen Elliott. 1862	11. Rev. Wm. E. Wyatt, D.D. 1829–1850
11. Bp. John Henry Hopkins. 1865	12. Rev. Wm. Creighton, D.D. 1853–1859
12. Bp. Stephen Elliott. 1865	13. Rev. James Craik, D.D. 1862
13. Bp. Benjamin Bosworth Smith. 1868–1883	14. Rev. Christian Hanckel, D.D. 1862
14. Bp. Alfred Lee. 1886	15. Rev. James Craik, D.D. 1865
15. Bp. John Williams. 1889–1898	16. Rev. C. C. Pinckney, D.D. 1865

PRESIDING BISHOPS	PRES. HOUSE OF DEPUTIES
16. Bp. Thomas March Clark. 1901	17. Rev. James Craik, D.D. 1868–1874
Bp. Daniel Sylvester Tuttle. 1904–1922	18. Rev. Alex. Burgess, D.D. 1877
17. Bp. Ethelbert Talbot. 1925	19. Rev. E. E. Beardsley, D.D. 1880–1883
18. Bp. John Gardner Murray. 1928	20. Rev. Morgan Dix, D.D. 1886–1898
19. Bp. James DeWolf Perry. 1931–1937	21. Rev. J. S. Lindsay, D.D. 1901
20. Bp. Henry St. George Tucker. 1940–1946	22. Rev. R. H. McKim, D.D. 1904–1910
21. Bp. Henry Knox Sherrill. 1949–1958	23. Rev. Alex. Mann, D.D. 1913–1922
22. Bp. Arthur Lichtenberger. 1961–1964	24. Rev. Ernest M. Stires, D.D. 1925
23. Bp. John Elbridge Hines. 1967–1973	25. Rev. ZeB. Phillips, D.D. 1928–1940
24. Bp. John Maury Allin. 1973—	26. Rev. Phillips E. Osgood, D.D. 1943
	27. Hon. Owen J. Roberts. 1946
	28. V. Rev. Claude W. Sprouse, D.D. 1949
	29. V. Rev. C. W. Sprouse, D.D. Rev. T. O. Wedel, Ph.D. 1952
	30. Rev. Theodore O. Wedel, Ph.D. 1955–1958
	31. Clifford P. Morehouse, LL.D. 1961–1967
	32. Rev. John B. Coburn, D.D. 1969–

SECRETARIES OF THE HOUSE OF BISHOPS AND OF THE HOUSE OF DEPUTIES, 1785–1975

SECRETARIES OF THE HOUSE OF BISHOPS	SECRETARIES OF THE HOUSE OF DEPUTIES
1. Rev. Joseph Clarkson 1789–1792	1. Rev. David Griffith 1785–1786
2. Rev. Leonard Cutting 1792–1795	2. Honorable Francis Hopkinson 1786–1792
3. Rev. Joseph Turner 1795–1799	3. Rev. John Bisset 1792–1795
4. Rev. John Henry Hobart 1799–1801	4. Rev. James Abercrombie 1795–1801
5. Rev. Henry Waddell 1801–1804	5. Rev. Ashbel Baldwin 1801–1804
6. Rev. Cave Jones 1804–1808	6. Rev. John Henry Hobart 1804–1811
7. Rev. Dr. James Whitehead 1808–1811	7. Rev. Ashbel Baldwin 1811–1823
8. Rev. Philo Shelton 1811–1814	8. Rev. John Churchill Rudd 1823–1826
9. Rev. Jackson Kemper 1814–1817	9. Rev. Benjamin Tredwell Onderdonk 1826–1832
10. Rev. Benjamin Tredwell Onderdonk 1817–1820	10. Rev. Henry Anthon 1832–1843
11. Rev. William Augustus Muhlenberg 1820–1823	

TREASURERS OF THE GENERAL CONVENTION

*Offices of Secretary of House of Deputies and Treasurer of the General Convention combined in 1970.

Prior to the meeting in Louisville in 1973, the General Convention had selected its next meeting site from one Convention to the next. Since, in its present form, the size and the needs of General Convention require the largest convention facilities in the United States, putting it in direct competition for this space with other conventions, it was necessary to take a longer look at the process of selecting future sites. The experience of the Committee on Agenda and Arrangements in planning the 1973 Convention indicated that several departures from past custom had to be made if the General Conventions of the future were to be successful ventures. The complex nature of Convention, as well as its size and duration, limits the possible places in this country where it can be held. There are other conventions that attract more people, but few that last as long or demand as much in the way of particular space requirements. The larger convention facilities capable of handling the General Convention of the Episcopal Church must be reserved from six to nine years in advance, making the previous selection process unrealistic. Therefore, with the Convention on a triennial basis, the 1973 General Convention voted to plan meeting sites at least three Conventions in advance. Consequently, in 1973 a firm commitment was made for the next three Conventions. The sixty-fifth General Convention (called "The Minnesota Convention") will meet in the Minneapolis/St. Paul, Minnesota Convention Hall in the Diocese of Minnesota; the sixty-sixth will meet in Denver, Colorado, at the downtown Denver Convention Complex; and the sixty-seventh will meet in Milwaukee, Wisconsin, at Mecca, the Milwaukee Exposition and Convention and Arena. The site for 1985 will be voted upon at the 1976 General Convention and will be presented to the Convention by the Committee on Future Sites. Since the selection of cities had to be made so far in advance, it was necessary to design a process guaranteeing that the facilities and hotels would be adequate that far in the future. This is discussed in detail in chapter 7.

Another change that occurred in 1973 was that the Convention is now planned, produced, and financed by the General Convention itself. The Convention meeting at Houston in 1970 was the last Convention to have a "host" diocese. The system of expecting dioceses to invite the General Convention to meet within their jurisdictions and to be responsible for financing all the expenses over the amount allotted in the General Convention budget became unrealistic. In recent years, the amount required of the "host" diocese was disproportionate and burdensome to the diocese, often necessitating the borrowing of funds.

Now, the choice of site, the planning, arrangements, management, and financing of the Conventions has become the responsibility of the Convention itself through its executive office. This is discussed more fully in later chapters: finances in chapter 6 and management in chapter 7.

It would be an impossible task to give a complete and accurate history of General Convention within these pages. However, the person attending General Convention is placed within a rich and varied history of prior Conventions. The new deputy or visitor should try to visit the diocesan historiographer and learn of those who have represented the diocese at previous Conventions, and then read past *Journals* of Conventions to become united in spirit with a long process of the evolving Episcopal Church in the United States and throughout the world. A rich history of the Church is also contained within the Episcopal Church Archives at Austin, Texas. One is certainly encouraged to contact the archivist and become familiar with the abundant heritage contained in the documents housed there.

With this brief history of General Convention serving as an introduction, let us now proceed to gain an understanding of the structure and process of General Convention. To attempt participation or observation of the meeting itself without such background is to experience complete frustration. These pages will help the participant as well as the observer, to become a part of General Convention from the first day of its meeting and to understand its actions and work throughout the succeeding triennium. Episcopalians may not always have been happy with the resolution of issues or with the manner in which they were disposed of—let alone with Convention leadership. But the genius of the Episcopal Church working through General Convention is that changes do come and issues are resolved. The time frame in which they occur may not be to everyone's liking, but historically the Church has effected change both within and without its structure. It is this working within the structure that has been most effective in bringing change. To understand the structure, then, and become a part of it is to be a responsible and effective person working within General Convention. That is the hope of the writer for all those who read this book.

CHAPTER 2

THE STRUCTURE
OF GENERAL CONVENTION

> . . . consisting of the House of Bishops and the
> House of Deputies.
>
> *Constitution—Article I, Section I*

It was apparent from the earliest time of the Church that it would
be an organized institution. It began when Christ chose the
twelve apostles and trained them during his ministry. However,
the discouragement and disillusionment suffered by the Twelve
after his arrest and subsequent crucifixion could have been disas-
trous. They were inclined to remain secluded within the walled
city of Jerusalem and to mourn over what might have been. It was
the genius of the ministry of Paul that caused Christianity to
cease being a "sit-ment" in Palestine and become a "movement"
throughout the world. Through his missionary journeys and
teachings on the continents of Asia and Europe, the "Good
News" of what had happened soon spread. And as it spread, bands
of believers met together to worship the Son of God in synagogues
and private homes.

As they became more involved they took on projects of minis-
tering to the poor, the widows, and the fatherless. The distribution of food and clothing among the needy soon made organiza-

tion a necessity, which, in turn, created problems of authority. Paul instructed these early followers of Christ about the organization the early Church should take. It was a simple form, yet it was vital to the future of the Church. These early years of Christianity are obscured, but it is known that the Church, due to the persecution of Christians, functioned as a viable underground organization. Rome was the world's political power and the many pagan deities recognized by the Roman emperors were pronounced the official objects of worship throughout the Roman world. It was upon the Roman roads, however, that the message of Christianity was carried to the peoples of other lands.

The message of Christ reached the shores of Britain early, perhaps as early as A.D. 208. Soon, the British were Christianized under missionary enterprise and, as early as the fourth century, the Church was functioning with bishops and priests. By this time, Rome had officially recognized the Christian Church and in A.D. 410, when the Roman army withdrew from Britain, Christianity was fully established.

The development of English government closely paralleled that of the early Church of England. Kingly rule was administered through the county sheriffs and local courts. Eventually, jurors were employed in the counties to enforce the laws of the kings. It was from this system that the House of Commons in Parliament would evolve. Meanwhile, as the Church in England developed, it was necessary for the bishops to meet in convocations and it was from these convocations that the representative form of parliament drew its pattern. From 1225 until the convocation of 1283, there was an evolution within the convocation of prelates of the Church that eventually included proctors, monastics, and archdeacons. By 1283, the convocation of Canterbury included bishops, abbots, deans, and archdeacons, together with two representatives from the clergy of each diocese and one representative from each chapter. It was on this full representation that King Edward modeled his Parliament of 1295 which became the form of Parliament known today in England. Thus, the Church had evolved a government for itself that was adopted by the state.

Since its inception, there had been a tendency in the Church toward absolute rule by one person—as in the case of the papacy —which resulted in internal tension within the Church structure. But throughout the history of the Church there has also been the desire for input by both clergy and laity. Just as the political governments of nations have desired a people's voice, so has the Church. In England, the pope's rule was replaced by that of the king's. Under the spiritual leadership of the archbishops, the bishops, clergy, and laity became involved in matters relating to the government of the Church. The convocation became a gathering of persons who represented all parts of the membership. Each had a voice. Yet, there was still allegiance to the king of England as the temporal head of the Church. It was this allegiance that created a problem for the early colonists that had caused the Church in America to separate from the Church of England.

The Church of England has undergone structural changes within its organized body as recently as 1970. It has changed from its historical bicameral body into a single unicameral "national synod" in which each diocese is represented in the three orders —bishops, clergy, and laity—by representation proportionate to diocesan membership. It is said that this has significantly limited the use of the time consuming vote by orders in the convocation, but it has increased the need for more frequent meetings of the General Synod of the Church of England.

The General Convention of the Episcopal Church is a bicameral legislative body, consisting of the House of Bishops and the House of Deputies, that studies itself and its structure through the Standing Commission on the Structure of the Church. It presents its report at every meeting of the General Convention and expresses its concerns in many areas of the organizational structure of General Convention. In 1973, these concerns involved clarifying the executive function of the Presiding Bishop and the function and responsibility of the Executive Council. The Commission was also concerned with the grouping of other committees, commissions, boards, and the General Convention legislative committees. Recommendations with regard to diocesan boundaries were also presented to the General Convention for consideration. As to the General Convention as a whole, the Commission made recommendations regarding representation of racial and ethnic minorities and youth, General Convention being held biennially, and other matters. This report is always awaited eagerly by persons attending General Convention, as it causes much discussion and debate. Generally, the open hearings and commission and committee meetings are well attended, and people seek to express themselves on both sides of the report and recommendations. A deputy to General Convention would be wise to study the report well in advance in order to be knowledgeable about the current thinking on the future structure of the General Convention as an organized body.

In speaking of the General Convention structure, the foregoing is what is generally referred to. However, it would be remiss to speak of structure without stating that the General Convention meeting itself is also structured. This structure is the agenda of the meeting for the thirteen days currently being used for the conduct of legislative matters and other concerns of the Church. Following is the tentative proposed schedule designed by the Committee on Agenda and Arrangements for the 1976 General Convention. There are many aspects to it and a careful study of the legislative calendar in chapter 4 will help orient the persons

attending General Convention as to some of its structured activities during the two-week period.

TENTATIVE PROPOSED SCHEDULE

SEPTEMBER 1976

8–9–10	Liturgical commission open hearings, Leamington Hotel
10	Orientation for new deputies
11	Opening Worship Service—4:00 P.M., St. Paul Civic Center
12	Worship in Minnesota churches and pulpit exchange
12	Organizational session in both Houses—3–5 P.M.
13–23	(except Sunday the 19th)
	Committee meetings—8 to 9:30 A.M.
	Daily worship—9:40 to 10:20 A.M.
	Houses convene—10:30 A.M.
	Lunch—approximately one and a half hours
	Afternoon legislative session—2:00 P.M.
	Open hearings—7:30 P.M. nightly except Friday and Satur-day, the 17th and 18th
17	Bicentennial Commission & Diocese of Minnesota to recognize the Presiding Bishop and the celebration of the nation
18	Legislative sessions end around 1:00 P.M.
	Less formal events, such as diocesan dinners, reunions, etc.
19	United Thank Offering Service—11:00 A.M. in the Arena
	Possible use of afternoon or evening by Program and Budget for presentation
20–23	Repeat schedule of first week with evenings being held for open hearings as issues develop

This is a tentative proposed schedule by the General Convention
Committee on Agenda and Arrangements. It is subject to change prior
to the opening of Convention and is not the official agenda until
adopted by both Houses, Sunday, Sept. 12, 1976.

One of the highlights of the General Convention is the opening worship service. This is a moving and spiritual experience

shared by 10,000 to 15,000 worshipers. Most of the people in attendance are those present for General Convention in an official capacity, visitors to Convention, delegates to the Triennial Meeting of the women of the Church, those attending other conventions and meetings within the fellowship of the Episcopal Church, and official observers and guests from other communions.

Prior to 1973, the opening worship service was planned by the local diocese in which General Convention met. At Louisville, this service was planned by a national committee appointed by the Presiding Bishop and the President of the House of Deputies. This was an attempt to include all viewpoints of liturgy and music within the expression of worship at General Convention. It was a large eucharistic service with a sizable central altar and some twenty-five satellite communion stations throughout the large convention hall. Following a procession of bishops, deputies, members of religious orders, and invited guests, the Presiding Bishop addressed the assembled worshipers and then was the celebrant at Holy Communion, with the bishop of the local diocese and others serving as the concelebrants. The elements were prepared by members of the clergy using communion vessels that were especially designed and made for that General Convention. Previously, the communion vessels had been borrowed from the local parishes. An opening Eucharist was first used at the Special General Convention at South Bend in 1969, and again at Houston in 1970. Prior to 1969, the opening service was a service of Evening Prayer.

The 1976 General Convention will have its opening worship service in the new 18,000-seat Civic Arena in St. Paul. It will take the form of a specially ordered worship service of hymn singing and preaching. Again, this service is under the direct responsibility of the Presiding Bishop, who is traditionally responsible for all worship activities of the General Convention. He appoints a committee-at-large to assist him in this very important aspect of the General Convention. The responsibility for the ordering of daily worship, which occurs every legislative morning in the Chamber of the House of Deputies from 9:40 until 10:20 A.M., also falls to the Presiding Bishop. It is for all participants and visitors at General Convention.

Another part of the General Convention structure that is important to its function is the exhibit area. This is a vital part of the General Convention as it provides a great portion of the money needed to underwrite the actual cost of the Convention. It is usually seen by some as being primarily a commercial venture. Without it, however, the cost of the Convention would be a greater burden to the Church. Since the General Convention is not an annual convention, there is little other opportunity for agencies of the Church, publishers, vestment manufacturers, church suppliers, and others to present their programs, ideas, and products to thousands of bishops, clergy, and lay people. The exhibit area is a highlight of the Convention for it brings several hundred exhibitors together under one roof, offers hours of interaction and a spell of relief from the Convention process itself. It is a welcome diversion for many.

"The Common Ground" is a place with which everyone attending a General Convention will want to become acquainted. It was originally designed at the South Bend Convention in 1969 as a place for the issues to be discussed in an informal atmosphere. It was so popular that it was again used at both the Houston and Louisville Conventions. A similar center for evening activity is called "The Gathering Place" and is located at the headquarters hotel. Both are places where people may meet and engage in conversations about the issues and matters before the General Convention. There is no entertainment at "The Common Ground" but there are tables and chairs, and people may have refreshments and conversation. "The Gathering Place," however, may have entertainment. It serves as a place of relaxation before retiring for the night.

The Triennial Meeting of the women of the Church is held concurrently with the General Convention. Though this meeting is separate from the General Convention, it has traditionally met at the same time, in the same city, and, if possible, under the same roof as the General Convention. The planning group is separate from that of General Convention but there is a close working liaison between the Triennial and the General Convention. The Triennial may present memorials directly to the General Convention for consideration. Triennial delegates pay the same registration fee as bishops and deputies as well as its proportionate share of the cost of the convention facility. It is attended by about five hundred to six hundred persons.

There is yet another aspect to the total structure of the General Convention meeting itself, and that is the number of other conventions and groups that meet either prior to or concurrent with General Convention. Persons attending these meetings may also serve later as deputies to General Convention or as delegates to the Triennial. Some of the groups are: The National Association of Diocesan Altar Guilds, The Daughters of the King, and the Church Periodical Club. There are other groups of the Church that generally meet for one day prior to the opening of General Convention. All of these put added stress upon the hotels and function areas of the convention city and require careful coordination by the General Convention manager.

Thus, the observer sees that there is a very carefully structured organization known as the General Convention of the Episcopal Church. He should also notice that the meeting itself is just as carefully structured.

CHAPTER 3

THE PROCESS
OF GENERAL CONVENTION

> . . . which Houses shall sit and deliberate sepa-
> rately; and in all deliberations freedom of debate
> shall be allowed. Either House may originate
> and propose legislation, and all acts of the Con-
> vention shall be adopted and authenticated by
> both Houses.
>
> *Constitution—Article I, Section I*

A General Convention of the Episcopal Church doesn't just
happen. It takes months of planning and preparation by committees, staffs, dioceses, and groups. Someone once said, "You can
search the world over and you will never find a monument erected
to a committee." However, if a monument ever were erected to
a committee, it should be to a committee of the General Convention of the Episcopal Church.

The committee process was reformed at the 1973 General
Convention to allow for greater discussion and complete consideration of the issues before it. Time had been the limiting factor
prior to that Convention. Because of the size of the House of
Deputies and the inordinate amount of work facing it once every
three years, an effective committee system was proposed by the
Committee on Agenda and Arrangements. Prior to 1973, the

organization of the committees normally waited until the opening of the General Convention. However, there was nothing in the Rules of Order preventing an earlier formation of the committee structure.

The committee procedure now in effect is presented here for a full and complete understanding of the process of General Convention. The report of the 1973 Committee on Agenda and Arrangements stated that any legislative body with a significant work load depends upon an efficient and effective committee system to permit maximum discussion and consideration of the issues before it in a minimum amount of time. This is particularly true in a body the size of General Convention, meeting as infrequently as it does and with the volume of business which it must handle.

The Committee on Agenda and Arrangements was convinced that certain reforms and alterations in the method of operation of the committees would greatly improve the efficiency of the Convention and permit a much more thorough consideration of all issues than would be possible under the practices that have prevailed in the past.

The annual appointment by the Presiding Bishop of committees and chairmen of legislative committees of the House of Bishops had been going on for several years prior to 1973. In 1973 the President of the House of Deputies was authorized to do the same.

Much of the material submitted to the Convention is available prior to the Convention itself. The committees of the Houses for which resolutions were filed prior to the Convention are called to meet on the two days before the formal opening to organize themselves for business and to undertake preliminary consideration of the material before them.

In the past, no specific time was allotted in the Convention schedule for committee meetings, nor were there specifically assigned places for the committees to meet. It was proposed that the hours of 8:00 to 9:30 A.M. each day be set aside for meetings of committees, and facilities were provided for such meetings. It was also proposed that, as far as possible, all committee meetings be open to visitors—that is, to other members of the Convention not assigned to that committee, to participants of the Triennial, and to visitors to the Convention. By prior registration with the chairman of the committee, any person may testify before the committee on any matter that it may be considering. Due provision has been made for executive sessions.

This process provides for a much simpler and more direct method of reporting the committees' recommendations to the Convention. Reports are made on standard forms and submitted to the secretary, who reports these findings to the respective Houses of the Convention. Nothing, it should be noted, prevents any committee chairman from speaking to the findings of his committee; the manner in which the various resolutions are brought before the Houses has simply been expedited.

The following guidelines were given to members of the Convention to familiarize them with this process. They are presented here for the readers' understanding. (It should be noted that the "Blue Book" referred to below is the booklet containing all prefiled documents which is mailed to bishops and deputies prior to each Convention.)

PROCEDURAL PROCESSES AND TOOLS TO FACILITATE COMMITTEE FUNCTIONS:

A. Time and place of committee meetings.

Prior to General Convention, each committee chairman will be provided with a designated time and a designated place for the regular meetings of his committee. He should hold to an absolute minimum the need for any special meetings of his committee at a different time or place. The time and place of meeting of each committee will be announced and publicly posted during the meeting of the Convention.

B. Notice of hearings.

Each day the chairman of each committee should provide the Secretary of the House of Deputies with three copies of Exhibit A attached hereto containing by assigned number (and Blue Book page reference, if applicable) the legislative proposals scheduled for hearing by the committee at its meeting on the following day. The Secretary will make an announcement of this notice and will post a copy thereof upon a bulletin board provided for the purpose in a public area near the chamber of the House of Deputies and at a general exit area from the meeting hall.

C. Witness identification and registration blanks.

Each chairman will be provided by the Secretary with a supply of Exhibit B (witness slips). He, or a designated member of his committee, should be at his assigned committee room and have available a supply of such slips approximately ten minutes before the scheduled time for his committee to meet in order that registration can be completed and witness scheduling can be planned in advance. No person who is not a member of the committee should be permitted to address the committee unless he has registered to do so.

D. Committee reports.

At the conclusion of each meeting of the committee, the chairman, or a specific person designated by him, should complete a set of Exhibit C forms with regard to each legislative proposal upon which the committee took final action during such meeting. Such a report should be explicit and should make only one of the following three recommendations:

That (no. of proposal) (Blue Book page____) be adopted;

That (no. of proposal) (Blue Book page____) be not adopted;

That (no. of proposal) (Blue Book page____) be adopted with the following amendment(s), to wit.:

(here reproduce explicit language of amendment in one of the
forms suggested in Appendix, page____).

Every committee report should be dated, signed by the chairman of
the committee, and transmitted to the office of the Secretary of the
House.

If a committee other than the committee on amendments to the
Constitution or the committee on Canons makes any recommendation
upon any legislative proposal involving an amendment to the Constitution or the Canons, the Secretary of the House shall immediately trans-
mit the same to the appropriate committee for review and approval of
the proposal as to form. The chairman of the committee to which such
proposal has been referred shall cause it to be considered by his committee as to questions of form only, shall endorse upon the committee report
the action of his committee on this question, and return it to the office
of the Secretary of the House.

The Secretary of the House shall report all committee reports to the
legislative sessions of the House.

No legislative proposal should be permitted by the chairman to remain in his committee without being made the subject of a report.

EXHIBIT A
COMMITTEE NOTICE

The Committee on_____will meet in
Room____, at____A/PM, on_____, 19____, to consider the
following legislative proposals:

      H.D. No._____(G/B/P____); No._____(G/B/P____)
      H.B. No._____(G/B/P____); No._____(B/B/P____)

_____
Chairman

This form should be filed in triplicate with the office of the Secretary
prior to adjournment of the House at least one day prior to the date of
the scheduled hearing.

EXHIBIT B

WITNESS REGISTRATION

The undersigned _____
                    (Deputy, Visitor, Other)

representing _____
              (Self, Organization, Group)

desires to appear and be heard by the Committee on
_____in connection with its considera-

tion of_____ _____
        H.D.__ H.B.__

Dated:_____

_____

EXHIBIT C

The Committee on_____has con-
sidered_____(which appears on p.____of the
Blue Book) and recommends

                That it be adopted·
        Strike That it not be adopted
          out   That it be adopted with the following
          two   amendment(s):

                (here insert the explicit amendment)

Dated:_____

                                        _____
                                        Chairman

APPROVED as to form
    Committee on Amendments to Constitution
    Committee on Canons

                                        By_____

Dated:_____

Because most of the resolutions being presented at General Convention have been prefiled with the Secretary and mailed in advance to the bishops and deputies, and because the chairmen have been oriented beforehand to the committee process, it is possible to have the various committees of both Houses meet in advance of the formal opening of General Convention for organization and the preliminary consideration of the matters before them. The committees are not permitted to make any final conclusions prior to the opening of General Convention in order to allow for full and open debate when the matter is presented to the full Convention.

For committees having an issue before them which requires more space and more free input, an open hearing may be scheduled. This is a special provision whereby persons are not required to register with the chairman before speaking on the subject before the committee. Usually, the chairman will ask that those having opposing views on the subject take their places on either side of the microphone and then have the alternating views expressed. The presentations are usually limited by time and by the freedom of expression desired. Open hearings are for the benefit of the full committee, as well as to allow for an open Convention process. Sometimes as many as two thousand persons have participated in an open hearing. The hearings are well publicized and are usually conducted in a large room or in the spectator seating area where the General Convention meets.

There are Standing Committees in the House of Bishops and the House of Deputies. Those committees having to deal with the same subject matter are called "cognate committees." They may meet separately or jointly. Each committee presents its business in its separate House. For a full understanding, they are presented here in parallel.

There may be, and generally are, other committees of the two

HOUSE OF BISHOPS	HOUSE OF DEPUTIES
Dispatch of Business	Dispatch of Business
Certification of the Minutes	Certification of the Minutes
Rules of Order, of which the Presiding Bishop shall be a member, *ex officio*	Rules of Order, of which the President shall be Chairman, *ex officio*
Constitution	Constitution
Canons	Canons
Structure	Structure
Admission of the New Dioceses	Admission of the New Dioceses
Consecration of Bishops	Consecration of Bishops
World Mission	World Mission
National and International Problems	National and International Problems
Social and Urban Affairs	Social and Urban Affairs
Church in Small Communities	Church in Small Communities
Evangelism	Evangelism
Prayer Book and Liturgy	Prayer Book and Liturgy
Church Music	Church Music
Ministry	Ministry
Education	Education
Church Pension Fund	Church Pension Fund
Church Support	Church Support
Ecumenical Relations	Ecumenical Relations
Miscellaneous Resolutions	Miscellaneous Resolutions
Privilege and Courtesy	Privilege and Courtesy
Pastoral Letter	State of the Church
Resignation of Bishops	Credentials
Religious Communities	
On Nominations and Elections	
The Presiding Bishop names the members annually and designates the chairman of each.	The President must appoint members no later than sixty days prior to the opening of General Convention. The chairmen are now being appointed several months in advance.

HOUSE OF BISHOPS	HOUSE OF DEPUTIES
The size of each committee will be from six to nine bishops.	The size of these committees is at the discretion of the President.

Houses. For example, at the 1973 General Convention the following were special committees appointed in the House of Bishops:

Advisory Committee to the House of Bishops
Ministry of the Laity
Pastoral Development
Interim Meeting
Nominate a Vice-Chairman of the House of Bishops
Committee of Nine
Office of a Bishop
Theological
Armed Forces
Christian Marriage
Nominating Committee for Court of Trial of a Bishop and Court
    of Review of a Trial of a Bishop.

The President of the House of Deputies may appoint study committees related to the work of the Executive Council as well as special committees he deems desirable to appoint. Special committees may also be ordered by the House of Deputies. In 1973, these were: Holy Matrimony and Ordination of Women to the Priesthood.

The working documents of the General Convention are called memorials, petitions, resolutions, and recommendations. A memorial is an information document calling the attention of the General Convention to a particular situation. It is usually accompanied by a petition, in resolution form, which asks the Convention to act upon the information contained in the memorial. Memorials and petitions come from dioceses and provinces. A resolution is a request for action by the General Convention. Resolutions are received originally from bishops or deputies (any member of the General Convention). Recommendations are included in reports to General Convention from joint committees, joint commissions, boards, and official agencies of the General Convention.

At least ninety days in advance of the opening date of General Convention, any diocese, missionary diocese, joint committee, joint commission, agency, or board of the Episcopal Church, or any diocesan or provincial Episcopal Churchwomen's organization may submit to the Secretary of the General Convention memorials, petitions, or resolutions. Prefiling of materials is quite essential, for no new business requiring concurrent action can be introduced into the House of Deputies after the third day, or into the House of Bishops after the fifth day without a two-thirds vote of the members present. Any bishop or deputy may prefile resolutions with the Secretary. The receipt of them from Episcopal Churchwomen's organizations is not specifically provided for in the Rules of Order. They have, however, traditionally been received and placed into the legislative process. In the past it has been preferred that the Episcopal Churchwomen make their recommendations through the Triennial Meeting of the women of the Church, and then introduce them into the House of Deputies through the appropriate Diocesan bishop or one of the appropriate deputies. This keeps the legislative process orderly by having all memorials and petitions coming from dioceses of provinces. However, the Triennial is privileged to submit directly to the House within the three opening days of Convention. No parochial organization—or any individual, clerical, or lay—can submit or institute documents directly to the General Convention.

The General Convention legislative process for these documents is that prior receipt of memorials, petitions, resolutions, and recommendations are referred to the appropriate committee of both Houses either for information or for consideration and action. If a document is presented during the meeting of the Convention, it must be made in writing, in duplicate, and given to the President or Secretary of the House of Deputies. These are then referred to the appropriate committee by the President; placed upon the legislative calendar at the discretion of the President; or, upon a two-thirds vote of the members present in the House of Deputies, the House may consider the matter immediately. Should the President refer the matter to a committee, the committee then reviews it, takes action, and submits it to the appropriate House. A vote is taken by that House on whatever action is requested. If concurrent action is required by both Houses, the matter is referred to the other following action in one. The same process then follows in the House to which the matter is forwarded. The work load of the 1973 General Convention was heavy. One hundred sixty-five resolutions were recommended by joint committees, joint commissions, boards, and agencies to the House of Deputies. There were also one hundred seventy-four memorials and petitions filed previous to Convention from the diocese and provinces of the Church and twelve prefiled members' bills from bishops or deputies. Subsequently, almost one hundred members' bills were introduced into the House of Deputies and a like number into the House of Bishops. The range of subject matter was wide. The amount of work required by each of the committees to combine, refine, and prepare for presentation to Convention in an orderly manner, after full and thorough hearings, was gargantuan. The dedication and singleness of purpose of bishops and deputies are truly commendable. All this legislative matter must be received, refined, heard, prepared, debated, voted upon, and then forwarded to the other House for concurrence. Since only ten legislative days are structured into the legislative calendar of General Convention, this is an impressive feat of management.

The General Convention has provided for the establishment of joint committees and joint commissions in which matters of business and concern are studied during the time between General Conventions. Thus, they have a continuity of function. A joint commission may have members who are not members of Convention. Appointments of bishops to the joint committees and commissions are made by the Presiding Bishop, while the President of the House of Deputies appoints the clerical and lay members. These appointments are made very soon after the conclusion of the meeting of the General Convention. It is also provided by Canon I, Section 2(e) that a member of the Executive Council be appointed to each joint committee and commission to function as a liaison with Council. The Presiding Bishop and President of the House of Deputies also serve as *ex officio* members of the joint committees and joint commissions. At the completion of their report and their recommendations to the next General Convention, and upon the completion of that Convention, it is considered that they have fulfilled their function and are discharged from their duties unless special provisions are made for their continuance. Some joint commissions, however, are "standing" commissions established by Canon or by the Rules of Order, and these do no need to be reconstituted triennially.

Let us follow this process to see how a matter might come before the General Convention from a particular parish. There are many subjects and concerns before the churches today. Among the most prevalent would be Prayer Book revision. Should a particular parish wish to address itself to this or any other subject, it would have a resolution prepared by the vestry, the women's group, or an individual for presentation to the annual meeting of the parish. If it is of such a nature that the annual meeting would not be convenient, a special meeting of the parish might be arranged. The resolution would then be presented to the body for its consideration. If it receives a majority vote, it would be forwarded to the annual meeting of the diocese where it may be presented for consideration; or, if there were other resolutions of a similar nature, it could be assigned to a committee. If the resolution received favorable action by the diocese, it would then be forwarded to the Secretary of General Convention for inclusion among the matters for presentation to the Convention. The resolution would then be printed, along with the many others received, and mailed out to the deputies in booklet form, and referred to the appropriate committee. Alternately, a parish resolution may be committed to one of the diocesan deputies to Convention or to the bishop, to be introduced as a member's bill.

The resolution we are following from a hypothetical parish and diocese would then be assigned to a committee. If it is the only one on a particular subject, the chances are that it will be presented to the Convention in its original form. If there are several resolutions on the same subject, the committee will attempt to include all of the concerns into a few or even a single resolution. After committee meetings, and perhaps open hearings, then the appropriate committee asks the Committee on Dispatch of Business to place the matter on the agenda, after which, proper announcement of its hearing is made. This can often draw a large gallery into the House where the matter is being heard. After ample debate, a vote is called and the matter is decided by the body. Should it pass, it is then forwarded to the other House for concurrence. Through this democratic procedure, every member of the Episcopal Church has the opportunity to present matters of concern before the entire Church for consideration.

For an understanding of how the process of General Convention works in each House, it is advisable to secure a copy of the Rules of Order in each House. These set forth in precise detail just how the daily procedure operates. For example, the Rules of Order for the House of Bishops set forth instructions for services and devotions, first day of session, daily orders, general rules, bishops in council, the election of the Presiding Bishop, nominations for missionary bishops, executive sessions, standing orders, standing resolutions, and offices of devotion. There are similar, though more lengthy and detailed, Rules of Order in the House of Deputies. Section A is the section on Rules of Order dealing with the placement of Holy Scripture in the House, the opening of the daily sessions, order of business, standing committees, joint committees, and joint commissions; the form and procedure for filing and presenting petitions, memorials, and resolutions; parliamentary procedure in the House; and other general regulations. Section B has to do with standing orders. There are also "Joint Rules of the House of Bishops and the House of Deputies."

A thorough understanding of these rules and how they apply in both the House of Bishops and the House of Deputies will serve one well in the participation and observation of a General Convention. The Rules of Order are to be found in the *Journal* of General Convention and should be required reading for a deputy. To understand the process of General Convention is to be able to function within that process effectively.

CHAPTER 4

HOW GENERAL CONVENTION WORKS

IN THE HOUSE OF BISHOPS:

Each Bishop of this Church having jurisdiction, every Bishop Coadjutor, every Suffragan Bishop, and every Bishop who by reason of advanced age, of bodily infirmity, or who, under an election to an office created by the General Convention, or for reasons of mission strategy determined by action of the General Convention or the House of Bishops, has resigned his jurisdiction, shall have a seat and a vote in the House of Bishops. A majority of all Bishops entitled to vote, exclusive of Bishops who have resigned their jurisdictions or positions, shall be necessary to constitute a quorum for the transaction of business.

The House of Bishops shall choose one of the Bishops of the Church to be the Presiding Bishop of the Church.

Constitution—Article 1, Section 3

IN THE HOUSE OF DEPUTIES:

. . . each Diocese which has been admitted to union with the General Convention shall be entitled to representation in the House of Deputies by not more than four Presbyters . . . and not more than four lay persons.

Constitution—Article 1, Section 4

. . . each missionary Diocese beyond the territory of the United States of America shall be entitled to representation in the House of Deputies equal to that of other Dioceses . . .

Constitution—Article 1, Section 4

There shall be a President . . . of the House of Deputies.

Canon, Section 1(a)

The General Convention of the Episcopal Church is composed of two legislative houses, as is the Congress of the United States. Our "senate" is the House of Bishops and our "house of representatives" is the House of Deputies. This two-house structure is known as a bicameral legislative body. The House of Bishops is attended by approximately 150 to 160 of the 230 active and retired bishops of the Church. From among the Church's 113 domestic and overseas dioceses, a potential 904 deputies and 904 alternate deputies are elected at diocesan conventions in the year preceding the year of each General Convention. Each diocese may elect four clerical deputies and four alternates from among its presbyters (clergy). They may also elect four lay deputies and four alternate lay deputies. The election is for the entire triennium between General Conventions. In the event of a special General Convention, which can only be called by the Presiding Bishop after consultation with the Executive Council, those deputies elected during that triennium would attend unless other deputies had been elected in the meantime. The persons elected as deputies must be residents of the diocese in which they are elected and they must be communicants of the Episcopal Church. Should General Convention so decide, there is a provision by Canon whereby this representation may be reduced to not fewer than two deputies in each order. This has not been the practice, however, because of the desire of the Church-at-large to have more, not less, representation at General Convention.

At the 1969 Special General Convention in South Bend, the respective dioceses were urged to send specially designated representatives to participate with the bishops and deputies in the discussion of the issues confronting it. This was repeated for the Houston Convention in 1970, but with a less definite indication of the categories from which the additional representatives were to be selected. The Convention of 1973 did not have special representatives, choosing rather to have more participation by the visitors. The Committee on Agenda and Arrangements felt that the presence of the additional representatives had been extremely helpful to the deliberations of the two previous Conventions but that the need of the Convention to hear opinions from persons other than bishops and deputies could be obtained through open participation in all General Convention activities, other than legislative sessions, by all visitors who choose to attend. Thus all visitors were given the privileges previously designated for the additional representatives. However, for the 1976 General Convention, the Committee on Agenda and Arrangements returned to the concept of special representatives followed at the Houston and South Bend Conventions. The appointments for these special representatives are made by the diocesan bishop, if he chooses to appoint them. If a person believes his particular minority or social action or cause has not been provided for in his elected deputation, he may petition the bishop to be appointed a special representative. Application does not necessarily guarantee appointment or expense money, nor does it provide voice, vote, or seat in the House of Deputies.

Expenses for attendance at General Convention are provided on a *per diem* or lump sum basis by each diocesan budget. This has become a very expensive but necessary item for the dioceses.

At present, General Convention meets for a period of thirteen days, and a hotel room and three meals can be quite expensive. Adding the air fare and other transportation costs, the basic financial outlay for one person attending Convention could be well over seven hundred dollars. Therefore, the number of deputies and alternates, as well as the special representatives and bishops being sent to General Convention, must be well planned financially by each diocese. Because of the cost to the dioceses, the numbers of persons attending Convention from overseas is usually minimal, and is either underwritten by companion dioceses in the United States or funds are provided through the Executive Council. As a result of the high costs there has recently been much discussion about the size and duration of the General Convention. Some people have suggested having a ten-day Convention and reducing the size of deputations from eight to six persons. The discussion also centers around having a biennial General Convention in order to stay abreast of current issues. The advocates of this idea feel that the agenda could be shortened by having fewer issues to confront at one time.

The proposed agenda, as recommended by the General Convention Committee on Agenda and Arrangements, is the first order of business at Convention in both Houses. It may be changed upon the floor of either House and upon concurrence by the other, and is not final until its acceptance. As shown in the chart (page 23), the agenda is the structure of the thirteen days, providing time for committee meetings and debates on the floors of both Houses. It also provides for the scheduling of the opening worship service, the activities of the organizational meetings of both Houses, the first week's legislation and committee meetings, the special events, a free weekend at the end of the first week, and then the final days of legislation.

Some committees of General Convention meet during the week preceding the opening day of Convention. The Convention committees may organize a day or two before Convention opens and prepare for the task before them. Some of the committees have budgets enabling them to meet throughout the triennium, such as the Committees on Program, Budget and Finance, Nominations, and Agenda and Arrangements. Open hearings may also be scheduled, necessitating the early arrival of interested persons, groups, and others. These open hearings are usually well publicized ahead of time.

One of the continuing problems of General Convention is that of orienting newly elected deputies to the process of General Convention. As many as sixty percent of the deputies in attendance may be there for the first time. Some dioceses conduct orientation and training sessions for several months prior to Convention, indoctrinating the deputies in the process and issues they will confront. Other dioceses have no training at all. However, several months before Convention, the pre-Convention booklet containing the recommendations of joint committees and commissions, boards, and agencies is mailed to the deputies for their information and consideration. Election to the General Convention deputation is one of the highest responsibilities given a member of the Church, and it should be a matter of integrity and stewardship on the part of each elected person to be prepared and well informed about all the matters to be deliberated by General Convention, as well as about its organization and process.

Some persons reading this book may have never been to a General Convention and may like to know how they might become involved. The answer may seem at first very flippant, simplistic, and elementary. But it is basic. Get yourself elected a deputy. How? By being involved actively in the work of the local diocese and by making your desire to serve as a deputy known to your rector, your vestry, your parish, your diocese, and your diocesan nominating committee. You must stand for election in the normal process within your diocese and be elected at your diocesan convention in the year prior to the General Convention you would like to attend. There are four regular seats on the floor of the House of Deputies for lay persons and four seats for the clergy. There is also the possibility of being elected as an alternate deputy. The only way the seat can be filled is by persons who make themselves available and who stand for election to them. It is difficult for some persons to take a regular vacation and be away from their occupations and homes for the two weeks necessary for General Convention. This, however, is what is required at present and is what is done by hundreds of concerned and dedicated clergy and lay persons at each General Convention.

Another way persons are involved—and this is generally done by those who live in or near the city in which the General Convention meets—is by serving as volunteers. Between 1,000 and 2,000 persons help by serving as ushers, pages, office staff, registration clerks, exhibit assistants, and in many other positions of responsibility. Volunteers provide an invaluable service to the General Convention and they also gain a very rewarding experience for themselves. Usually volunteers are from the diocese of the Convention site and are chosen about nine months prior to the opening date. Volunteers are also sought from among the contiguous dioceses.

Visiting General Convention is another way a person can participate. Persons living a reasonable distance from the Convention city are encouraged to visit some of the sessions. Usually thousands of visitors attend General Convention. They are permitted to sit in the Visitors' Galleries of both Houses and hear the debates and discussions on the floor. Seating charts, by which bishops and deputies may be identified, are provided. A registered visitor may also attend, and even speak, at open hearings. The visitor has access to the large exhibit areas where work and ministry of various Church-related organizations and agencies, vestment manufacturers, church furniture companies, and many more interesting exhibitors are to be found.

If the distance to General Convention is too great, a person can participate in it by other means. A subscription to *The Episcopalian,* a monthly newspaper containing Episcopal Church and Church-related news, is quite helpful. *The Convention Daily* is published at General Convention by a news gathering staff and copies can be received by mail at a nominal subscription price. A telephone answering service containing a summary of each day's proceedings is usually available. The telephone number is published ahead of time and a person, diocese, or parish can, for the price of a long distance call, be given daily reports of Convention activities directly. Of course, one's local press may carry details of General Convention but usually only the more spectacular issues are covered and this does not help the interested Episcopalian to catch the real flavor of the proceedings. This is also true of the national publications.

Let us now turn our attention to the Houses of General Convention.

THE HOUSE OF BISHOPS

The seating arrangement of the House of Bishops is compact. But there is a comradery and familiarity here that lends itself to a lower key of excitement than that which is found in the House of Deputies. There is also a sense of continuity here. The House of Bishops meets at least once each year, thus enabling the bishops to have a continuing fellowship over the years.

Bishops, traditionally, are seated in the House of Bishops in the order of their consecration to the episcopate. Consequently, the newly ordained bishops are seated to the rear of the House and affectionately referred to as "baby bishops." In recent years, however, this seating arrangement has not always been adhered to because some of the senior bishops have not enjoyed being up front and having to turn around to observe the participants during a debate. Each seating place is provided with a desk blotter, a glass, a pitcher of water, and an ashtray. (Smoking is permitted in the House of Bishops, while it is prohibited in the House of Deputies.) Microphones are conveniently placed around the seating area so that those bishops desiring to address an issue or subject may do so and be heard by all. Usually there is a closed circuit television camera placed in the House carrying the live proceedings to the press room, Executive Council information area, and the Common Ground. There is also a large press area that serves as a divider between the bishops and the public.

The raised platform at the front of the House has desks upon it for the Presiding Bishop, the Secretary of the House of Bishops, and his assistant. A rostrum stands in front of the platform for speakers who wish to address the bishops from the front of the House. There are also several seats behind the desks for distinguished guests who may be there to observe or to address the House.

The business of the House of Bishops usually proceeds in quite an orderly fashion. The several committees of the House meet in assigned rooms and then report their findings to the Committee on Dispatch of Business which places it on the agenda. All sessions of the House are open to the public except during the nominating speeches and the process of electing a Presiding Bishop. The election of a Presiding Bishop provides for nomination in the House of Bishops with concurrence in the House of Deputies. Since the General Convention of 1967 in Seattle, election is for a twelve-year term of office.

The following table shows the names and tenure of each Presiding Bishop since the first General Convention in 1789. The numbers in parentheses after the names refer to their order of consecration as bishops.

A TABLE OF PRESIDING BISHOPS*

1. WILLIAM WHITE (2) (Bishop of Pennsylvania), from July 28, 1789, to October 3, 1789.

2. SAMUEL SEABURY (1) (Bishop of Connecticut), from October 5, 1789, to September 13, 1792.

3. SAMUEL PROVOOST (3) (Bishop of New York), from September 13, 1792, to September 8, 1795.

4. WILLIAM WHITE (2) (Bishop of Pennsylvania), from September 8, 1795, to July 17, 1836.

5. ALEXANDER VIETS GRISWOLD (12) (Bishop of the Eastern Diocese), from July 17, 1836, to February 15, 1843.

6. PHILANDER CHASE (18), (Bishop of Illinois), from February 15, 1843, to September 20, 1852.

7. THOMAS CHURCH BROWNELL (19) (Bishop of Connecticut), from September 20, 1852, to January 13, 1865.

8. JOHN HENRY HOPKINS (26) (Bishop of Vermont), from January 13, 1865, to January 9, 1868.

9. BENJAMIN BOSWORTH SMITH (27) (Bishop of Kentucky), from January 9, 1868, to May 31, 1884.

10. ALFRED LEE (38) (Bishop of Delaware), from May 31, 1884, to April 12, 1887.

11. JOHN WILLIAMS (54) (Bishop of Connecticut), from April 12, 1887, to February 7, 1899.

12. THOMAS MARCH CLARK (63) (Bishop of Rhode Island), from February 7, 1899, to September 7, 1903.

13. DANIEL SYLVESTER TUTTLE (84) (Bishop of Missouri), from September 7, 1903, to April 17, 1923.

14. ALEXANDER CHARLES GARRETT (108) (Bishop of Dallas), from April 17, 1923, to February 18, 1924.

15. ETHELBERT TALBOT (143) (Bishop of Bethlehem), from February 18, 1924, to January 1, 1926.

ELECTIVE

16. JOHN GARDNER MURRAY (243) (Bishop of Maryland), from January 1, 1926, to October 3, 1929 (died in office).

17. CHARLES PALMERSTON ANDERSON (197) (Bishop of Chicago), from November 13, 1929, to January 30, 1930 (died in office).

18. JAMES DEWOLF PERRY (247) (Bishop of Rhode Island), from March 26, 1930, to serve until General Convention of 1931. Reelected September 25, 1931, at General Convention held in Denver, Colo., for a term of six years to end December 31, 1937.

19. HENRY ST. GEORGE

A TABLE OF PRESIDING BISHOPS (cont'd)

TUCKER (258) (Bishop of Virginia, resigned** in 1944), from January 1, 1938, to December 31, 1946.

20. HENRY KNOX SHERRILL (372) (Bishop of Massachusetts, resigned June 1, 1947), from January 1, 1947, to November 14, 1958.

21. ARTHUR LICHTENBERGER (503) (Bishop of Missouri, re-signed in 1959), from November 15, 1958. Resigned for ill health. October, 1964.

22. JOHN ELBRIDGE HINES (461) (Bishop of Texas, resigned December 31, 1964), from January 1, 1965 to May 31, 1974.

23. JOHN MAURY ALLIN (581) (Bishop of Mississippi (resigned 1974) From June 1, 1974–.

*NOTE.—The title *Presiding Bishop* was not used in the Journals of General Convention until 1795. This Table is based on the premise that the Bishop who was President of General Convention or of the House of Bishops before 1795 was *de facto* Presiding Bishop.

The General Convention of 1789 during its first session (July 28–August 8), and for the first five days (September 29–October 3) of its second session (September 29–October 16), consisted of one House only. Bishop White was *President of the General Convention* throughout its first session and for the first five days of its second session, and as such signed the minutes of the first session.

When, on October 5, 1789, a separate House of Bishops was first organized, Bishop Seabury became President of the House of Bishops in accordance with the rule of seniority, based on the date of consecration to the episcopate.

On September 13, 1792, Bishop Provoost became President of the House of Bishops by the adoption of the rule that the office should "be held in rotation, beginning from the North."

In 1795, under the above rule, Bishop White automatically became President of the House of Bishops, and for the first time the title *Presiding Bishop* appears in the signing of the minutes of that House. In 1799, "the Bishop whose turn it would have been to preside" not being present, "Bishop White was requested to preside." In 1801 the rule of rotation was suspended. On September 12, 1804, the rule of seniority was again adopted and continued in effect for 115 years.

The General Convention of 1919, by amending the Constitution, provided for the election of the Presiding Bishop by the Convention. The first election of a Presiding Bishop under the new provision took place at the General Convention of 1925.

**NOTE.—At present the Presiding Bishop is chosen from among the Bishops but must resign his own diocese when he assumes his new office—or within six months. He is elected for twelve years, beginning twelve months after the close of the General Convention at which he is elected, or until the Convention after he is sixty-five. (See Canon II.2 for further detail.)

*From the *Episcopal Church Annual, 1976.* Copyright 1976, Morehouse-Barlow Co. Used by permission.

The House of Bishops is another means whereby a member of the Church can be involved in General Convention. Consultation, personal conference, or correspondence with a bishop about an individual's opinions on subjects before the General Convention can often be helpful to the bishop and to his vote. He is free, of course, to vote as he sees fit on any subject or issue before the House, and consequently before the whole Church. Many times a bishop will caucus with the deputation from his diocese on certain matters. These caucuses are usually held at the various hotels, and some have been known to last until the early hours of the morning if a vote is to be taken on a sensitive subject the following session. This is a contributing factor to the extreme tension endured by the participants of General Convention during its two weeks of meetings.

The actions of the House of Bishops are recorded by the Secretary, who is elected by that body at the opening session. Usually, the first order of business is to establish whether a quorum for voting exists in the House. The guide for this certification is to be found in Article I, Section 2 of the Constitution. As the business of the House proceeds, it is often difficult to know just when a matter will be reported out of committee and presented upon the floor for the debate. Hence, the astute observer at General Convention will keep a close watch on the order of business and be sensitive to situations as they develop within that body.

THE HOUSE OF DEPUTIES

By referring to the floor plan of the House of Deputies, it is at once evident that this is a larger and more complex House than the House of Bishops. At present, seats for 904 deputies are provided at tables. The selection of a place upon the floor for a deputation is not by design, as in the House of Bishops, but rather in a random drawing for seats conducted by the Secretary or his designate. Large placards placed atop ten-foot-high steel poles serve as identification for each particular diocese. Eight chairs are provided for a deputation; however, these are not in a straight line. Seating is according to orders. Four clergy deputies from a diocese are seated at one table in the row nearer the platform, while the four lay deputies are seated immediately behind the clergy of their deputation.

This provides for consultation and easier communication among the deputation during the conduct of business in the House.

The large 30- by 40-foot platform at the front of the House of Deputies contains several desks and a number of guest chairs. Seated at the desks are the President, who serves as the presiding officer; the Secretary and assistant secretaries, who record the proceedings, verify a quorum present at each session, and take each vote for recording; the chairman and some members of the Committee on Dispatch of Business, charged with the order of the agenda at each session; and the Parliamentarian.

The large panorama of the House of Deputies, with all that it represents, is indeed breathtaking. Its size and procedural sound can be awe inspiring, while its actual debate is sometimes frustrating. Nevertheless, it is the voice of the Church in action. From the sound of the opening gavel, through each often heated debate, to the close of each session, one is led to feel that "this is where the action is."

When an item has been reported out of committee and placed upon the agenda of the House of Deputies by the Committee on Dispatch of Business, open debate begins after its introduction into the House. Nine microphones are placed throughout the House of Deputies at small platform risers with numbers on them for easy identification. After recognition from the main platform by the President, a deputy may speak for or against the matter before the House. Lengthy debate is usually the order for those matters of extreme importance. These may be scheduled at a specific time as a special order of business. When lengthy debate is required, those deputies wishing to address themselves to the matter are invited by the President to come to the front of the House and form lines on either side of the small platform. Usually, those in favor of the matter will form a line to the right, and those against to the left. From this position the persons wishing to address the House then speak alternately. A timer light is located on the rostrum which indicates how much time is left for debate on the subject. It looks rather like a small traffic light with vertical red, green, and yellow lights. If, for example, a deputy is allowed three minutes for presentation of his views on a subject, the Secretary will set the timer for three minutes. This activates the green light on the front of the rostrum. When only thirty seconds remain for the speaker, a yellow light appears and the green light goes off. This is the indication that the speaker had better begin the conclusion of his remarks. When time runs out for the speaker, the red light turns on and the speaker should conclude his remarks immediately. This, however, has not always been the case. On numerous occasions, the President has had to interrupt speakers in mid-sentence and ask them to stop.

When ample time has been given for the opposing viewpoints on a subject, a vote is taken among the deputies present. There must be a quorum present for the vote, which can be a simple "yes" or "no" voice vote, by a show of hands, or by a standing vote. Some issues (amendments to the Constitution or to the Prayer Book, for example) must be decided by what is called a "vote by orders and dioceses." Any issues, upon the request of a single clerical or lay deputation, may also be so decided.

The vote by orders and dioceses is an unfamiliar process to most deputies and requires clarification. In such a vote the House is deemed to consist, not of 904 individuals, but of 113 clerical and 113 lay diocesan units and a concurrent majority in the affirmative is required to adopt a resolution. Upon the calling of a vote by orders and dioceses, each deputation must caucus to determine its vote, which may be "yes," "no," or "divided" (if the four deputies vote two and two in the caucus). To pass requires fifty-seven affirmative votes in each order. It is often said that a "divided" vote counts as negative, but this is not strictly accurate; it is neither affirmative nor negative, but it is a vote reckoned in the total.

The House of Deputies' Committee on Rules of Order is proposing a method whereby each vote taken at the 1976 General Convention will be recorded, having the name and diocese of each member of the House electronically recorded together with each vote taken. This information will be available for printing in the *Journal* of General Convention. This elaborate procedure will permit a diocese to know exactly how each of its deputies voted upon each issue. This will allow, for the first time in the history of General Convention, accountability by individuals. It could be called the stewardship of the vote.

Voting for elective offices, including Executive Council membership is a lengthy and complicated procedure. In the past, it was done by tallying individual written ballots. At present, the vote to elective office in the House of Deputies is accomplished electronically through the use of a small punch-out tabulation card which allows a deputy to use a pencil point or other pointed object to punch out a small numbered tab that has a corresponding name which is announced by the Secretary. When instructions for voting by this method are given by the Secretary, each deputy should pay careful attention. Many good votes can be lost through carelessness and inattention.

Visitors are not allowed on the floor of the House of Deputies except at the special invitation of the President. This even extends to the Presiding Bishop, who needs an invitation to enter the House. No special permission is needed for the Visitors' Gallery.

Alternate deputies may be seated only if the regular deputy surrenders the badge to the Committee on Credentials and receives the badge of an alternate. The regular deputy may be seated again only when the regular badge is returned by the alternate to the Committee on Credentials. It is being recommended that this be done only once a day, and the alternate deputy must sit with his or her deputation. In the past, some deputies and their alternates have been quite active in exchanging their seats which proved confusing to the Secretary and became burdensome from the standpoint of determining the quorum and make-up of the House.

Joint sessions of the House of Deputies and the House of Bishops occur in the House of Deputies chamber because of its greater size. These are generally for the opening session of the first day, and for the reports of the Executive Council and the Standing Committee on Program and Budget. At these sessions an extra chair is placed at each deputation for each bishop of the diocese. At the close of a joint session, the bishops' chairs are removed from the floor.

Information and communication are provided in the House of Deputies by several means. Distribution boxes are placed upon tables at a convenient place upon the floor of the House. Since the unauthorized placement of the printed matter at the deputies' seats is forbidden by the Rules of Order, it is only through the placement of authorized materials in these boxes that information is distributed to the deputies. These items are only those necessary to the conduct of business, such as printed resolutions, petitions, and memorials. Copies of each of the items of business for that session are placed in the boxes by volunteers working out of the Secretary's office.

Messages or notes between deputies, as well as between deputations, are delivered by volunteer pages serving in the House of Deputies. These volunteers are the only persons other than deputies allowed on the floor and who have freedom of movement during the conduct of business.

A large movie screen is placed to one side of the platform and, from time to time, has projected upon it messages of an emergency nature for individual deputies. The screen is also used for general announcements, such as the location of committee meetings. Also, at the close of each session, the Secretary may announce the place and time of meeting for committees of the House that are scheduled for that day, that evening, or the succeeding morning. These meetings are scheduled with the office of the committee meetings coordinator, who also places a notice of meeting immediately outside the House of Deputies and in the *Convention Daily*. Forty to fifty meeting rooms are required for the meetings of the House of Deputies and the House of Bishops. They are of various sizes and are located throughout the Convention Hall. These rooms are controlled by the committee meetings coordinator, a responsibility established for the 1973 General Convention. Meeting rooms are generally assigned for the duration of the Convention. If, due to the number of persons attending, a room is too small, another may be assigned. This is also done for the opening hearings.

Closed circuit television is also provided from the House of Deputies to the press room, "The Common Ground," and the Executive Council consultation area. This has proved a useful aid in observation of the Convention in both Houses for persons desiring to take a break from the proceedings. This is especially true for the press corps. It enables them to be in the press room and yet, when the action starts in one of the Houses, to know of it immediately and make a dash for the press table of either House.

The press is generally present in large numbers for each session of the House of Deputies. They are seated in a special section with tables provided for their note-taking. Electrical outlets are also provided for those reporters desiring to record the proceedings. At the 1973 General Convention over 350 reporters were registered and given credentials. These included Associated Press, United Press International, Reuters, *Time* magazine, *New York Times, Washington Post,* and many others from throughout the world, as well as representatives of diocesan papers. General Convention is an important news event and is usually reported on a day-by-day basis. A large Convention support staff, under the direction of the Executive Council communication staff, directs this undertaking. Daily briefings are conducted in a press briefing room on the topics under current discussion in Convention. Sometimes the leaders of the debate, as well as the officers of both Houses, are present for these briefings. In this way the local and national newspapers become a source for the flow of information out of General Convention back to the dioceses and members of the Church.

The first week of General Convention consists of a morning session and afternoon session daily in each House. Beginning at 10:30 A.M. and continuing until about 12:30 P.M., both Houses meet simultaneously. After a recess for lunch both Houses reconvene around 2:00 P.M. and continue until around 5:30 P.M. Seldom is an evening session scheduled the first week of legislation, although this usually becomes necessary the second week if the agenda is in danger of not being completed. In the past, some sessions have continued until after midnight. This has become less possible due to the legislative process developed for Convention by the 1973 Committee on Agenda and Arrangements.

Prior to 1973, and since General Convention met in Hawaii in 1955, the legislative calendar had not permitted sufficient time for the full debate of matters before the Convention, which resulted in unfinished business. Because of the unfinished business of the Church and because of new concerns, a special General Convention was called by the House of Bishops for 1969, which met at South Bend on the Notre Dame campus. Looking back, the observer of General Conventions can see a definite change in the style of the Convention at St. Louis in 1964. Prior to that Convention the triennial meeting of the Church had been more like a family reunion, a fraternal gathering, a vacation. There were times of stress and tension, but it was a hard working legislative Convention confronting the hard issues of the day. The Convention met in auditoriums and sat in theatre style seats.

It was at Seattle in 1967 that tables were first arranged in a classroom style and deputies were seated on one side of the tables facing the platform. This permitted a place for all of the papers, notebooks, reference books, and other resource items necessary for each deputation to function. Formerly, all materials were held upon each individual's lap resulting in great inconvenience and the loss or dislocation of materials.

Unfortunately, this change in physical set-up did not help expedite the legislative process. The problem lay in several areas. It was apparent that too much time was being given to floor debate in order to have ample airing of all sides and persuasions of the issues. This did not allow, however, for input from persons who were not deputies and who felt left out of the process. Great emotion often built up within those persons and groups because they felt their voices were not being heard. Several attempts were made at these Conventions by unofficial persons to interrupt the proceedings. This did occur, for example, at South Bend in 1969. The charge was that it was a closed Convention. But how could the process be opened up and still permit ample time for input of all persons and issues? How could a process be created to allow for openness?

It was apparent that the size of both Houses was rapidly increasing and that there was more demand for debate time upon both floors—more so in the House of Deputies than in the House of Bishops. More resolutions, memorials, and petitions were being presented and the pressure placed upon the triennial process was building up to the point that some solution had to be found. At the Louisville Convention in 1973 an answer was found. It lay in an idea called "The Stochastic Process," which was put forward by the chairman of the 1973 Committee on Agenda and Arrangements, Dr. Bruce Merrifield (deputy from Western New York). Through his leadership and the technical application of a committee member, Mr. James Winning (deputy from Springfield), the process of General Convention was opened. The committees had previously met in places and at hours not convenient for large numbers of visitors and observers. Also, many of the committee meetings were not open to the Church-at-large.

COMMITTEE PROCESS

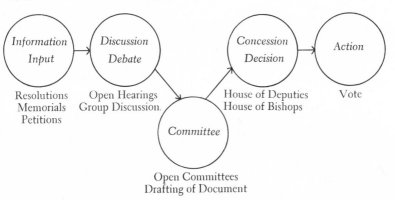

Following the diagram, one can see that there was ample opportunity under this arrangement for the issues to be debated prior to a matter being introduced into either House. This had been the frustrating and time-consuming factor. Matters were discussed in committees and then debated on the floor often without adequate input from differing and opposing viewpoints. Naturally, there was great anxiety on the part of visitors and observers to Convention. Now a person can attend a committee meeting and, after registration with the chairman on an appropriate form (see chapter 3), address the matter of a larger viewpoint in the drafting of legislative matters. Also, the floor debate is shortened because the matter has usually had a full airing prior to reaching the floor of either House. Consensus is usually gained in a more effective and less confusing manner.

Everything that occurs within the Episcopal Church as a whole is usually reflected in General Convention sooner or later. It is the manner in which the Convention deals with the issues before it that determines the anxiety level within the Church. The way the Convention works has been designed for maximum effectiveness and openness. To work within that framework guarantees that all sides of an issue will be heard. If it is done in the manner for which it was designed—people being given a chance to be heard —it works.

CHAPTER 5

THE ROLE OF
THE EXECUTIVE COUNCIL
IN GENERAL CONVENTION

> There shall be an Executive Council, whose
> duty it shall be to carry out the program and
> policies adopted by the General Convention.
> *Title 1, Canon 4*

There has often been confusion in the Episcopal Church as to
what the function and responsibility of the Executive Council is
and what its role consists of in the life of the national Church.
Many persons have thought that the Executive Council is the
governing body of the Church and that the General Convention is the servant of the Council. The opposite is true. The
General Convention is the creator and the Executive Council is
the implementor. To put these two in their proper perspective,
one should think of the General Convention as policy and the
Executive Council as program. In other words, as Canon 4
stipulates, "The Executive Council shall have charge of the
unification, development, and prosecution of the Missionary,
Educational, and Social Work of the Church, and of such other
work as may be committed to it by the General Convention." It
goes on to say, that "The Executive Council shall be account-

able to the General Convention and shall render a full report concerning the work with which it is charged to each meeting of the said Convention."

Each General Convention, therefore, has a place and time in its agenda for the proposal of a general Church Program for the next three years from the Executive Council and for election to seats on the Council. The Report of the Council is made to a joint meeting of both Houses, and takes between one and two hours to present. It is a highlight of General Convention because it is an indicator of the direction the Church has taken in the preceding triennium and will perhaps take in the succeeding triennium. The report is usually contained in an attractively bound notebook that is presented to each bishop and deputy of General Convention. This report must be mailed out to each deputation at least four months prior to the opening of the Convention in order that the various activities of Executive Council may become familiar to all bishops and deputies. This joint meeting of both Houses has many visitors seated in the Visitors' Gallery listening to the report of the work and the ministry of the Episcopal Church. The entire membership of the Executive Council is usually seated on the platform and taking part in the presentation of the report.

Elections to the Executive Council occur in the separate Houses. Persons elected to a seat on Executive Council may be elected by the General Convention itself for a six-year term of office. After that period, three years must elapse before that person becomes eligible for re-election. The General Convention also elects persons to Executive Council to fill vacancies caused by death, resignation, or change of ecclesiastical status. A second method of election to a seat on Executive Council is done by Provincial Synod. Each of the nine Provincial Synods has the right to elect one member at its regular meeting before General

Convention. The term of office for the person elected from the Provincial Synod is three years.

The composition of the membership of the Executive Council elected by General Convention is six bishops, six presbyters, and eighteen lay persons, making a total of thirty members. Three bishops, three presbyters, and nine lay persons are usually elected at each General Convention. This may vary due to vacancies that have occurred. Because of the importance of the work and ministry of the Executive Council, and the need for well qualified persons from within the Church to serve on it, there is a Joint Committee on Nominations which, among its other responsibilities, nominates persons for the Executive Council. This committee solicits names and biographical sketches from among the Church-at-large of persons deemed capable of serving on Executive Council. After the committee has received the nominations and met for consideration of the candidates presented to it, a report is presented to General Convention naming its selections. The two Houses may vote on these. Nominations may also be made from the floor of either House. The bishops are elected by the House of Bishops and the presbyters and lay persons are elected by the House of Deputies. Each election is subject to confirmation in the other House. The term of office for elected members begins immediately upon their confirmation and their written acceptance, which must be filed with the secretary of the Executive Council.

Should a vacancy occur within the membership of the Executive Council between General Conventions, or should a priest be consecrated a bishop or a lay person become ordained, the vacancy is filled by the Executive Council itself. A person thus elected may fill the vacancy until an election can occur at the next General Convention. If a vacancy occurs within the Executive Council among those elected by the Provincial Synods, the presi-

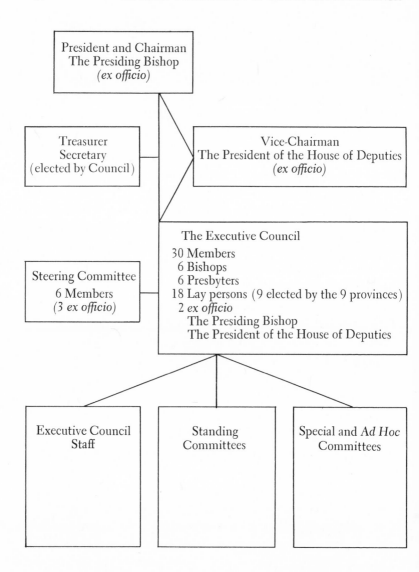

The Executive Council Organizational Chart

dent of the synod and the Executive Council of the province appoints a suitable person residing in that Province to serve until the expiration of that term of office.

The Executive Council exercises the powers given to it by General Convention and is governed in its powers by the Canon Law of the Church. Between the sessions of General Convention, the Executive Council may initiate and develop new work which it believes necessary to the ministry of the whole Church and to the extent its anticipated income warrants. It may enact bylaws to govern itself and the departments or programs under its supervision. The Presiding Bishop serves as president and chairman of the Executive Council while the President of the House of Deputies serves as vice-chairman. Both are *ex officio* members of the Executive Council. The Council itself elects the vice-presidents, the secretary, and the treasurer. Its organization may be like the one shown in the diagram (page 64).

In order to fully understand the Executive Council and its task, it must be realized that the Council is structured into committees which function and report back to the Council. It also directs the work of the Executive Council staff, officed primarily at the Episcopal Church Center, 815 Second Avenue, New York, N.Y. The concept of oneness in ministry to the Church is being greatly emphasized during this triennium by the Presiding Bishop. He is attempting to have the work of the Executive Council staff be one of ever widening circles reaching out from the resources of the staff into the provinces, the dioceses, and the parishes. Each division of the Executive Council staff has an executive and support staff. The finances for the program and support of the staff are part of the budget Executive Council presents at each General Convention. The personnel staffing resources usually change emphasis or direction at each triennial meeting of General Convention.

A reading of the present special and *ad hoc* committees of the Executive Council indicates the areas of ministry and concern of the General Convention at present.

> Community Action and Human Development
> Compensation
> Ghetto Loan and Investments
> Episcopal Asiaamerica Strategies Task Force
> Episcopal Commission for Black Ministries
> Management of Records and Documents
> National Commission for Hispanic Affairs
> National Committee on Indian Work
> Social Responsibility in Investments
> Structure
> Trust Funds
> Youth and College Ministries

These committees may have staff personnel employed outside of the regular Executive Council staff, or they may employ staff consultants for assistance in the accomplishment of their various tasks, assignments, and ministries.

The Standing Committees of the Executive Council are:

> Steering
> Communication
> Development
> Ecumenical
> Education
> Evangelism
> Finance
> Lay Ministries
> Mission Service and Strategies
> National and World Mission
> Personnel
> Social Ministry and Concerns
> World Relief, Board for Presiding Bishop's fund for

The reader must note that these committees are separate entities from the committees of General Convention. Though there may be similarities of concerns, and the reports out of each may be similar, the committees of the Executive Council are for the Executive Council work throughout the triennium while the work and reports of the committees of General Convention are solely for the work of the General Convention, enabling its legislative process to function and give direction to the work and ministry of the Executive Council. This does not imply that input and information is not utilized by the committees of both Houses; it is merely an attempt to point out the separateness of the committee structure in Executive Council from that in General Convention.

The Executive Council also acts in another capacity. It serves as the Board of Directors of the Domestic and Foreign Missionary Society of the Protestant Episcopal Church in the United States of America (PECUSA), which was established in 1821 by an act of the state legislature of New York. The Society is inclusive of all members of the Episcopal Church. It is this part of the Church for which the Executive Council legally has direction for the finances, and the disposition and overseeing of the money and property of the Episcopal Church. It is the Society that is the legal recipient and custodian of all funds given, willed, and entrusted to the Church for the furtherance of its work.

The Council submits a Proposal for a General Church Program for each Triennium, together with a budget. This proposal is prepared in consultation with the dioceses.

In 1972, teams made up of Council members and other Church leaders, together with staff, made special visits to virtually every diocese for advice. The results were recorded in the bulky publication *What You Said,* and summarized in the pamphlet

What We Learned from What You Said, which was given wide distribution throughout the Church. The priorities identified through this visitation process were maintained in the proposal made at Louisville in 1973.

In preparation for the Minnesota Convention in 1976, each diocese was asked if it wished another visit. Few dioceses considered this necessary, although many invited a Council member or Council staff member to sit with them informally in their own program planning in order to indicate their priorities for national Church programs and services.

Representatives of the more than fifty agencies and commissions which sponsor programs funded by the national Church are also invited to submit their requests to the Executive Council both in writing and in special hearings early in Convention year. The deputies' workbook for the 1973 Convention included transcripts of each of these written presentations, together with other supportive and explanatory material.

Before both the 1973 and 1976 Conventions, the Executive Council has presented its proposal at meetings of each of the nine provinces. These meetings, usually held in May and June of Convention year, provide an opportunity for bishops, deputies and alternates, together with Triennial delegates, to have an early introduction to the proposal and to ask questions for clarification. Their comments are helpful in the final presentation of this proposal at Convention.

These province meetings also provide invaluable training for delegates who have been elected to the Convention for the first time.

The Executive Council is also required by Canon to submit a report of its stewardship during the three years immediately before Convention. In 1973 this report was submitted to each delegate in the same workbook which contained the Council's proposal and was also printed and distributed separately. In 1976, distribution is being made through an illustrated sixteen-page insert in *The Episcopalian.*

In order to prepare the budget for presentation to General Convention, the Executive Council transmits to the president of each province a statement showing the appropriations to each diocese within each province and detailing just how the Executive Council program appropriations are spent within each jurisdiction. This is done at least fifteen months prior to General Convention in order that any changes may be made with the advice of the province so affected. The provincial synod, or executive council of each province, then considers the budget submitted by the Executive Council and reports its findings back to it.

From this input, the Executive Council then prepares the budget it presents to the General Convention for consideration in the underwriting of the programs and ministries of the National Church. At least four months prior to General Convention the bishop of each diocese receives a statement of the current budget and a copy of the proposed budget. At General Convention the Executive Council also submits, together with the proposed budget, a plan for the apportionment need from among the dioceses for the underwriting of the programs proposed.

This is the point at which every person who is a member of the Episcopal Church has the full recognition of participation in the whole Church through individual gifts of money given through a local parish. Each diocese is apportioned a share of the proposed budget, and the individual dioceses apportion their shares among the various parishes of their jurisdiction. All Episcopalians have a share in the work of the National Church through apportionment. This is the reason for the interest and the attendance at the session of General Convention where these matters are presented.

After presentation and full discussion of the proposed budget from the Executive Council, it awaits adoption by the General Convention. Following that, the Executive Council then has the power and authority to expend the sums of money that are covered by the budget and estimated for the programs and ministries approved by the General Convention, or for subsequent programs and ministries undertaken by the Executive Council. Upon the budget's adoption, the Executive Council advises each diocese just what its proportionate share of the budget will be in underwriting the Church's program adopted at the General Convention. The plan of underwriting is determined by the Executive Council on an equitable basis among the dioceses. After the various dioceses have received notification of their apportionment share from the Executive Council, they notify their parishes and missions of the objective amounts to be raised. In the diocesan presentation to the parishes and missions there is also included an apportionment for the budget of the diocese. The budget of each parish is then threefold: the local parish, the diocese, and the national Church.

The amounts of money budgeted by the Executive Council, not only for the national Church's program and ministry but also for diocesan programs and budgets, are considerable. Careful reporting of the receipts and expenditures of these funds is required. For example, every missionary bishop who receives financial aid from the Executive Council must report back to Executive Council on his stewardship at the close of every fiscal year. He is accountable for his work, the amount of money received from all sources and disbursed by him, and what the state of the diocese under his jurisdiction is at the time of his reporting. Every bishop receiving financial aid from Executive Council must also report on the work he is performing during the year in which he is being supported in whole or in part by money budgeted from the Executive Council. Upon the receipt of these reports, the Executive Council publishes a full report to the entire Church as to its works during the prior fiscal year. Its accountability contains an itemized statement of all receipts and disbursements, as well as a statement of all trust funds and property under its possession or control. It also reports on the salaries of its officers, agents, and principal employees.

In recent years, there has been concern about the total steward-ship of the human and financial resources being fully realized within the Episcopal Church. The 1973 General Convention resolved, "that the Office of Development of the Executive Council be directed to arrange visits and consultations with repre-sentatives of parishes, dioceses, the national Church, and others, for the purpose of developing a strategy to release the human and financial resources of the Church, and to report its findings and recommendations to the Presiding Bishop and Executive Council in February, 1975," and "that the Executive Council be author-ized and encouraged, on the basis of its findings, to implement such a strategy for the Church" (Resolution A–165). Both Houses concurred, and it will be upon the work of Executive Council in areas such as this that the program direction and implementation of the Church's future ministry depends.

When the budget of the Executive Council is presented, there is usually quite a lengthy floor debate. Proponents of certain areas of concern attempt to increase appropriations while those op-posed to these areas try to reduce the appropriations or cut them out of the budget altogether. It is a lively debate and one that should interest all members of the Church. The amount of money involved is considerable, running into millions of dollars. For example, the budget considered in 1973 was for over thirteen million dollars.

Another function of the Executive Council is in the field of appointment of missionaries. Ordained ministers and lay communicants of the Episcopal Church must qualify for appointment in accordance with the standards and procedures adopted by the Executive Council. There is also provision within the Executive Council that members in good standing of a Church not in communion with the Episcopal Church may be employed and assigned to positions for which they are professionaly prepared and receive the same stipends and allowances as appointed missionaries.

In order to facilitate its work, the Executive Council customarily meets four times each year, usually at Seabury House in Greenwich, Connecticut. Its proceedings are reported in the various news media throughout the Church, and those persons interested in the ongoing work of the program, ministry, and finances of the Church should read about each of these meetings. That way, the interested person will see just what the Church is doing, and how it is going about doing it, throughout each triennium. It is impossible to keep abreast of all the programs and concerns of the Church simply by attending a General Convention. Church ministry at the national level is provided for through the efforts and stewardship of the entire Church membership.

The Canons of the Church provide that:

There shall be an Executive Council, whose duty it shall be to carry out the program and policies adopted by the General Convention. The Executive Council shall have charge of the unification, development, and prosecution of the Missionary, Educational, and Social Work of the Church, and of such other work as may be committed to it by the General Convention.

The Executive Council shall be accountable to the General Convention and shall render a full report concerning the work with which it is charged to each meeting of the said Convention.

Title 1, Canon 4, Section 1(a),(b)

This, then, is the role of the Executive Council in General Convention. To understand it, know about it, and observe it is to move from a parochial viewpoint of Church membership to a broader spectrum of awareness that is so desperately needed in the Episcopal Church today.

CHAPTER 6

THE FINANCES
OF GENERAL CONVENTION

In order that the contingent expenses of the
General Convention . . . may be defrayed, it
shall be the duty of the . . . Diocesan Conventions to forward to the Treasurer of the General
Convention . . . a sum not greater than the
diocesan levy established by the General Convention.

Title 1, Canon 1, Section 8

At every regular meeting of the General Convention a Treasurer shall be elected . . .

Title 1, Canon 1, Section 7(a)

Every regular triennial meeting of General Convention elects a
Treasurer. The office is for three years and the incumbent may
succeed himself. Under the authority of the General Convention,
the Treasurer receives and disburses all of the collected moneys
of the Convention. He may even, with the advice and approval
of the Presiding Bishop and treasurer of the Executive Council,
invest surplus funds which may be on hand from time to time.
This has not been done in recent years, however, as the funds
necessary for the underwriting of the General Convention operat-

ing budget have been the victim of spiraling costs and economic factors.

At each General Convention the Treasurer is required to give an account of his stewardship during the preceeding triennium. His report is audited by an audit committee prior to its presentation. The Treasurer is also required to submit a detailed budget for the forthcoming triennium. That budget, which is prepared in consultation with the Joint Standing Committee on Program, Budget and Finance, is a detailed budget covering all areas in which the Treasurer anticipates future expenditures during the triennium. That committee is composed of six bishops appointed by the Presiding Bishop, six clergymen, and twelve lay persons who are appointed by the President of the House of Deputies.

The Standing Joint Committee on Program, Budget and Finance was created at the 1970 General Convention by the merging of the former Joint Committees on Program and Budget and of Expenses, and serves in an advisory capacity in conjunction with the Finance Committee of the Executive Council. Hence, the two committees serve to coordinate the financial structure of the two bodies. The Joint Standing Committee receives from the Executive Council the proposed budget for the triennium, as well as detailed annual budgets and biennial budget projections. These budgets are reviewed and adjusted annually. The triennial budget is presented by Executive Council to this committee at least four months prior to the regular meeting of General Convention. The committee meets in the next Convention city usually four to six days prior to the opening of General Convention in order to consider the budget requests and proposals and to conduct open hearings on the budgetary matters before it. The task of the committee is monumental, and it is an undertaking that continues right through the General Convention meeting. It requires hundreds of hours and long sessions before the final budget report is presented to the Convention itself. It is this committee that determines the diocesan requests for the annual apportionments.

The report of the committee and the task before it is, therefore, one that every Church member should have a great interest in, for it affects every parish, diocese, and the entire Church.

The budget presented to the General Convention for its consideration and adoption contains two parts. Part I is the section on expenses and is often referred to as "The Assessment Budget." It is financed by a levy established by General Convention upon every clergyman canonically resident within each jurisdiction. This also includes missionary clergymen. For example, the assessment rate for 1974 was fifty-three dollars for each diocesan clergyman and thirteen dollars and twenty-five cents for each missionary diocesan clergyman. This amount can change from year to year up to a ceiling established by Convention to meet the anticipated budgets presented to the committee. This budget pays for a portion of the actual cost of the General Convention meeting. (The balance of money needed for the General Convention meeting itself is derived from registration and exhibitor fees, which will be discussed later in this chapter.) It also pays the expenses of the office of the Presiding Bishop, as well as the expenses for staff and advisory council of the office of the President of the House of Deputies. Also included are the amounts for the House of Bishops, the House of Deputies, and the various committees, commissions, and societies of the General Convention.

Part II of the budget is the General Church Program Budget and is often referred to as the "Quota" or "Apportionment Budget," since this is the source of its funding revenues. For example, each diocese was apportioned a share of what was adopted for 1974, 1975, and 1976. Over thirteen million dollars was voted for the General Church Program. These amounts anticipated by the

General Convention were then forwarded by the various dioceses of the Church to the Treasurer on the first Monday of each January. This is necessary for the smooth flow of finances in the ongoing work of the General Convention.

There is usually considerable floor debate for budget presentation. This is where present programs of the General Convention are reviewed for continuance, and where programs currently being underwritten may be revised, or eliminated altogether. New programs may be included as well. It is usually a lively session and one that should be attended by those interested in the life of the Church, the current direction its ministry is taking, and the concerns it has for the world. As this is a world of continual change, these programs change continually. The flexibility and foresight needed is demanding. Nothing is binding or permanent on the General Convention. Programs and personnel can be changed. It is up to the concerned person to see that these areas for programing and expenditure are reviewed and structured to obtain the best results. This is the reason for the annual and triennial review of the program and budget of General Convention.

All of the foregoing has been a discussion of the methods of financing the organization. Let us now turn our attention to the methods of financing the event of General Convention.

The Seattle Convention in 1967 voted that it would accept the invitation of the Diocese of Florida to meet in 1973 in the city of Jacksonville. In 1970, the Houston Convention renewed the acceptance of that invitation. There soon developed an increasing awareness and understanding on the part of the members of the Convention that new factors, not previously of great importance, must now be kept in mind in planning for a General Convention meeting. By 1973, the size of the House of Deputies was increased by almost 200 members above the number present in

Seattle. The presence and participation of persons in discussion groups at both South Bend and Houston increased the number in attendance and represented a trend toward opening the Convention to fuller involvement by members of the Church. The informal gathering of persons at the Convention proved helpful to the full discussion of issues, and this trend could not be reversed. The numbers of young persons at recent Conventions, and of people of all classes and circumstances, demanded a wider variety of housing facilities, convenient access to the convention hall itself, and inexpensive meals.

At the meeting of the Committee on Agenda and Arrangements in Jacksonville, April 1971, that committee reluctantly reached the conclusion that the increased size and altered nature of the Convention itself, together with the changed housing situation that had resulted with the closing of several downtown Jacksonville hotels, made it unlikely that the facilities available in Jacksonville could conveniently accommodate the 1973 Convention. After many months of searching, the committee recommended to the Presiding Bishop that the 1973 General Convention meet in the Diocese of Kentucky in the city of Louisville. Acting with the advice and consent of the Executive Council, as provided in Title 1, Canon 1, Section 3, the Convention was moved from one diocese to another for only the second time in the history of the Church. (The first occurred in 1955 when the General Convention was moved from Houston to Honolulu.) Under the circumstances, it was necessary to assure the Diocese of Kentucky that the full cost of the General Convention would be borne by the General Convention itself, rather than shared with the "host" diocese.

Thus, by 1973 the Convention site was no longer a matter of diocesan invitation and there was no longer a "host" diocese except in the informal sense of cordial welcome by the diocese in which General Convention would meet. Funds are no longer required from the local diocese, other than those expended by choice of that diocese. Because of an emergency situation, the entire method of financing and management of General Convention was historically changed. The "host" of General Convention became the General Convention itself.

COMPARATIVE TOTAL COSTS OF GENERAL CONVENTIONS FROM 1961 THROUGH 1976

	TOTAL COSTS	COST TO NATIONAL CHURCH	COST TO DIOCESE
1961 Miami	$103,401	$ 21,562	$ 21,316
1964 St. Louis	$154,171	$ 15,856	$ 26,997
1967 Seattle	$202,293	$ 50,000	$ 58,565
1969 South Bend	$ 77,706	$ 77,706	None
1970 Houston	$380,827	$147,600	$148,117
1973 Louisville	$297,801	$150,000	None
1976 Minneapolis	$200,000 (est.)	$175,000	None

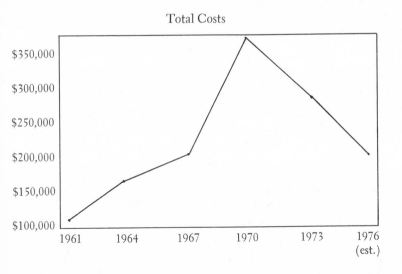

Total Costs

Now that the General Convention pays the entire cost of the Convention meeting, the financial burden that had previously been required of the local diocese is considerably relieved. For example, the total cost of General Convention facilities and arrangements rose 368 percent during the nine-year period from 1961 to 1970. By 1976, the cost to the General Convention rose from $50,000 to $175,000. It should be remembered that this covers only a portion of the cost of a General Convention meeting. The other sources of revenue come from registration fees and exhibitors' fees. By studying the graph on page 79, you will notice that the total costs of General Convention facilities and arrangements had been escalating. In 1973, the time at which General Convention became an event paid for and managed by itself, the cost of facilities and arrangements took a dramatic downturn. The actual cost to the General Convention had tripled over the previous $50,000 figure, and yet the cost to the local diocese was nothing. Because of negotiations that are constantly being reviewed and updated by the General Convention Manager, the trend shown should continue downward to a manageable level, even in these times of inflationary spiral.

In 1961 the proportionate share of the cost for a General Convention meeting was on a 50–50 basis. As the cost of all items related to General Convention, including labor, began to rise in 1964, the financial burden on the "host" diocese also became greater. The largest amount of money ever paid by a diocese for a General Convention meeting was in 1970 by the Diocese of Texas for the Houston General Convention. Consequently, an additional $100,000 was appropriated by the General Convention itself to help defray the expenses incurred by the diocese. This was to become the basis for the budgetary item now included in Part I of the Budget on Expenses. In 1973, under the direction of the manager, an all-time record in exhibit sales, registration fees, and departmental charge-backs was reached. This money, together with the $150,000 appropriated, resulted in an "almost-paid-for" Convention. There was only a $17,000 deficit after all bills for all events had been paid, which was absorbed by the General Convention itself. There was no long-term indebtedness required by the diocese, and shortly after the close of the Convention all accounts had been settled. With modern accounting methods now in effect in the General Convention executive office, the projected costs of the meeting can be identified and are indicated in the downward trend shown in Graph A. When the cost of the meeting is borne by the meeting itself, and diocesan money can be used for diocesan programs, this is good stewardship. It is not a wise expenditure of funds, nor is it sound stewardship, for one diocese to underwrite what should be the responsibility of the whole Church. Therefore, the amount of money needed for the conduct of the meeting itself has been included in the Assessment Budget of General Convention. This portion (currently $175,000) of the almost $200,000 required for a meeting is apportioned to the various dioceses, while the balance is the responsibility of the manager through the collection of the registration and exhibit fees.

All in all, the General Convention is being funded and managed effectively for the proper conduct of its business. It is only by understanding just how the change has come about and how it has had a positive effect upon the total stewardship of all its various parts that the work necessary for its conduct can be fully appreciated. Many feel that General Convention is now on the proper financial basis and that its affairs are in order. It certainly can be said that a dangerous financial trend has been averted and that the affairs of its management are on a businesslike basis. It is certainly of serious concern to

Episcopalians, both clergy and lay, that the affairs of the Church be conducted in a businesslike and efficient way. It can now be reported that in the case of General Convention they are so conducted.

CHAPTER 7

THE ADMINISTRATION
OF GENERAL CONVENTION

The administrative offices of General Convention were restructured in 1973. Prior to the Convention in Louisville, the Secretary-Treasurer had functioned *de facto* as the Executive Officer, having been assigned the tasks of attending and reporting on the meetings of all committees of General Convention, overseeing all the finances of the General Convention, attending to the budget preparation, arranging the coordination of all matters pertaining to the actual meeting of each General Convention, taking the minutes of each Convention and incorporating them into the agenda for publication and reporting, and editing and publishing each General Convention *Journal*. Because of the growth of General Convention and the number of bishops being consecrated each year, the need was apparent for relief in some of the areas being served by only one person.

In 1973 the House of Deputies proposed, and the House of Bishops concurred, that the General Convention Executive Office include two additional persons: the General Convention Executive Officer and the Manager of the General Convention. The office of the Secretary-Treasurer, already in existence at the time, is also included in this action by combining the three functions into what is now called the Executive Office of General Convention (see diagram on page 85). These three offices are separate in function and yet are interrelated in purpose.

The Executive Office of General Convention is headed by an Executive Officer appointed jointly by the Presiding Bishop and the President of the House of Deputies. His function is to oversee the work of the Secretary-Treasurer and the Manager, and to be responsible for the total functioning of the Executive Office. Additionally, the Executive Officer meets with the various committees and agencies of General Convention making periodic reports on their activities to the presidents of the two Houses. The Executive Officer also meets with the Joint Committee on Program, Budget and Finance, assisting in whatever way may be required in overseeing the budget of General Convention and the Executive Office. A report is given by the Executive Officer to the meetings of the Executive Council and generally covers the activities of the Executive Office during the period between the Coun-

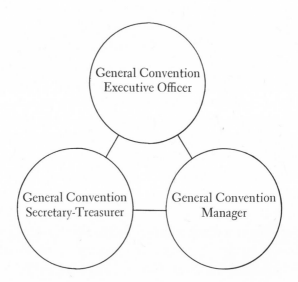

The Executive Office of the General Convention

cil's meetings. This is an evolving responsibility and one that has helped in the coordination of effort in the responsible and effective work of General Convention.

The position of Secretary-Treasurer, the second person within the Executive Office of General Convention, has become a full-time occupation with headquarters at the Episcopal Church Center in New York. The duties of the Treasurer have already been described in the preceding chapter. We now turn our attention to the duties of the Secretary, which are many and quite varied. This leads to a very complex function and one demanding the greatest accuracy, as the Secretary is charged by Canon with keeping the full minutes of the proceedings of the General Convention meeting and reporting them in the *Journal* of General Convention. This large volume is then distributed throughout the Church several months after the meeting. A copy of the preceding General Convention's *Journal* should be required reading for the new deputy.

In it will be found all the reports of the joint committees, joint commissions, boards, and agencies of General Convention, as well as the concurrent actions by both Houses. The *Journal* also includes a directory of the General Convention containing the officers of the Convention; the courts for the trial and the review of the trial of a bishop; the joint committees, joint commissions, and boards of General Convention; and the membership of the Executive Council. It also has the organization of both Houses with a list of the officers, roster, and journal of the House of Bishops and the officers, roster, committees, chairmen, and journal of the House of Deputies. Special meetings of the House of Bishops during the preceding triennium, the Rules for Order for both Houses, the Joint Rules of Order, and the Constitution and Canons of the national Church are all contained in the *Journal*. It can be readily seen that this book of over 1300 pages is a

marvelous source of information and should be absorbed by anyone desiring to participate fully and knowledgeably in a General
Convention. The cost of printing the *Journal* is sizable, and good
stewardship would require that it be used as a handy and ready
source for the clergy and lay person in roles of leadership within
the Episcopal Church.

The Secretary is required to keep the journal of the House of
Deputies and combine it with the journal of the House of Bishops, and he is also required to keep a record of the House of
Deputies for the registrar of the General Convention. This is a
complicated task involving checking credentials of those persons
qualified to sit at seats in the House of Deputies. Every vote in
the House is recorded by the Secretary for the permanent record.

The office of the Secretary of General Convention receives the
certification of election by diocese, notifying him of the names of
the clerical deputies and their alternates and the lay deputies and
their alternates. These are attested to by the secretary of the
diocesan convention, council, synod, or convocation. The Secretary's office then enters into correspondence with these persons regarding their preparation to attend the General Convention to which they were elected.

The Secretary is seated upon the platform of the House of
Deputies for the performance of his duties at a General Conven-
tion and is quite active and involved in its proceedings. The
Canons also provide that the secretary of the House of Deputies
may serve as *ad interim* President should both the President or
Vice-President be incapable of performing duties. The Secretary
could serve in that office until the next Convention or until such
incapacity is removed. Provision is also made for the office of the
Secretary to continue should a vacancy occur during a recess of
Convention. The duties of the Secretary may fall to the First
Assistant Secretary, as provision is made in the Canons for the

Secretary to appoint assistant secretaries to help in his tasks. If there is no First Assistant Secretary, the President of the House of Deputies appoints a Secretary *pro tempore.* Should there be no President or Vice-President, the members of the House of Deputies serving on the Joint Committee on Agenda and Arrangements for the next Convention may appoint a Secretary to serve until an election can be held. The election of a Secretary at every General Convention must have concurrence in both Houses.

The third person within the Executive Office of the General Convention is the Manager. This office was created at the General Convention meeting in Louisville in 1973 to fill a need created by the move away from the "host" diocese concept to a General Convention planned, produced, and financed by the General Convention itself. The Office of the Manager, together with the offices of the Executive Officer and the Secretary-Treasurer, is instrumental in giving guidance and leadership continuity to the Committee on Agenda and Arrangements and the Committee on Program, Budget and Finance for the sound planning of each triennium. The Office of the Manager was created to become, in fact, a function that the local "host" diocese previously served. This allows for the General Convention to take place within dioceses where it once would have been impossible due to the financial burden on the diocese. Because there are many who feel that a General Convention meeting within a community is a tremendous witness to that community and one that has a positive and lasting effect which remains long after the adjournment of the meeting, this is an important side effect to the General Convention meeting itself. The Office of the Manager assures General Convention that it will not have to revert back to the concept of the "host" diocese and the consequent financial burden; nor will it need to exclude any dioceses from having the Convention within its jurisdiction because of that burden. There is also the further positive effect of having continuity and continual guardians of the very important business aspects of General Convention. It also places the Church on a businesslike basis with proper cost control and management throughout the triennium.

The Office of the Manager is continually busy not only in the areas of planning, producing, and coordinating all aspects of a General Convention meeting, but from forty-five to fifty meetings of the various committees, commissions, and boards of the General Convention and Executive Council. This service has also been utilized by many groups within the Episcopal Church itself, ranging from groups numbering as few as ten persons to over 1500. By lowering the cost of meetings for those groups utilizing the service, it has been an effective means of stewardship.

The actual management of General Convention is a very complex operation involving many areas. Perhaps it could best be viewed through a verbal montage of activities necessary for the conduct of a General Convention. That would include upgrading procedures and designs of previous Conventions; budget management and projections; and negotiations with convention halls, hotels, caterers, decorators, telephone companies, transit companies, airlines, suppliers, and purveyors. The preparation of creature comforts at a General Convention requires many months of detailed planning and intricate arrangements for the utilization of 3,000 hotel rooms and for sleeping and feedings thousands of Episcopalians for a period that is, including time for pre- and post-Convention meetings, about thirty days. Notebooks, registration packets, and procedures need redesigning; and exhibit sales, brochures, kits, follow-up correspondence, and telephone calls are of utmost importance. Planning with individual groups for their own conventions, when these occur at the same time as the General Convention, takes much time and hard work. Preliminary work with each diocese as to physical arrangements, or any special activity it may desire is necessary to the success of arranging a Convention. Now the leaders of such groups have continuity in planning and arrangements. The organization and enlisting of a volunteer corps to serve at a General Convention, as well as the training of volunteers, comes under the leadership of the manager's office.

The recommendation of future sites for the General Convention also comes under the auspices of the Manager's Office. After a full and complete visit by the Manager and staff, a recommendation is made to the Executive Officer, who in turn forwards the Manager's choice to the Presiding Bishop and the President of the House of Deputies for concurrence. If that is obtained, the selection is forwarded to the Committee on Agenda and Arrangements for recommendation to the House of Deputies' Committee on Future Sites which, in turn, presents it to the House for action. As the choice of sites is no longer by diocesan invitation, the bishop in whose jurisdiction the Convention selects must be willing to have the General Convention meet within his diocese. It is carefully explained to him that General Convention is not asking for an underwriting of the cost, that any funds expended by him are solely a matter of his own choice, and that all the details of producing, planning, and managing the General Convention are under the Office of the Manager.

With the full staffing of the Executive Offices, the work load —both within the staff itself and the dioceses in which General Convention meets—has been more equitably distributed and efficiently managed. The burden to the local diocese has been greatly lessened, although there will always be anxiety and excitement where Convention meets. The General Convention should be an inspiration and a cohesive factor in the life of a diocese, not a despairing and divisive one. The overall result of this time of transition is that General Convention has assumed control of what is rightfully its own meeting, as well as full responsibility for it in every aspect. A careful study of the graphs in chapter 6 (pages 79) will indicate that the financial management of General Convention, through the efforts of the Executive Office, has created stronger stewardship and a more equitable cost basis. This should illustrate that the direction of the organization is correct and that its efficiency should continue to be a molding factor contributing to the effective stewardship and life of General Convention.

CHAPTER 8

THE FUTURE OF THE
GENERAL CONVENTION

> The Church has important work to do, God's
> work of redemption and reconciliation.
> *The Pastoral Letter of 1973*

General Convention is the arena where the impact of the world is met head on by the Church. It is the place where special causes and the concerns and cares of individuals or groups are presented for action. As long as there are problems in this world, General Convention will have a full agenda. There are issues before it that have been debated and discussed from one succeeding Convention to another; and there will be others.

One issue that is continually being discussed is the frequency of meeting. In a jet-lag world, where distances are diminished between nations and continents, and where miles are measured in minutes and hours due to the speed and convenience of air travel, it is possible to have more frequent meetings. Persons are transported quickly from one place to another with a regularity not known before the last twenty years. It is an age where great historical events, be it the inauguration of a President or the assassination of a President, are constantly before the populace through newspapers, television, and radio. The issues and concerns of the world are brought into every home daily and create an awareness of current events never thought possible when General Convention was first formed in 1789. The world moves swiftly, issues develop rapidly, and life seems to move ever more quickly.

Because of this, there has developed within the last few years a feeling in some sections of the Church that the General Convention can no longer afford the luxury of meeting only triennially. If it is to confront the world's problems and seek solutions to those problems, it should meet more frequently. Perhaps, instead of meeting and discussing issues every three years, every two years would be more reasonable. This has been put forward on occasion in documents prepared by the Standing Commission on the Structure of the Church. The main objection to this proposal is that some feel there would be an increased cost to the dioceses resulting from the increased frequency of meeting. The commission has suggested that this could be offset by reducing the size of the deputations from eight to six deputies, and by shortening the duration of the Convention.

Those proposing a biennial General Convention have defended the idea by suggesting that the debating of issues on a more current basis would help shorten the time of debate; and that an agenda with only two years time span would perhaps not be as crowded as an agenda covering three years of proposed legislation. They feel it would also make the Church more relevant to matters facing the world population. Events develop rapidly and it is not always possible for the Church to have an official opinion on matters of grave import. Should such a matter develop directly after the close of General Convention, an official statement of the Episcopal Church would have to wait for three years. A Special General Convention could be called by the Presiding Bishop, but this is a rare procedure and would add considerably to the overall cost of General Conventions.

The size of Convention has also become something of a general concern. At its inception it was a relatively small group that could meet in a single church and conduct its business accordingly. Because of the hospitality of parisioners and the small size of the groups, housing the deputations presented no immediate problem. Over the years the size of General Convention has become enormous and is destined to grow even larger. With the addition of only one diocese, the number of seats in the House of Deputies grows by eight persons. There has been some concern that the House of Deputies is becoming too large and unwieldy, and that there should be a reduction in the number of deputies in each deputation.

This would lower the cost to dioceses because of fewer persons to be transported and maintained throughout the Convention period; with fewer deputies to be heard, the length of debates would be considerably reduced. General Convention sites would be easier to select because of reduced space requirements; and committee size, floor space, and sleeping requirements would all be reduced proportionately. Simply in terms of the task of presiding over the House of Deputies, there would be great merit in reducing the size of the House, if only so the debates and discussion on the floor would be easier to handle. Of course, some voices in the Church—voices of those deeply concerned about the issues and the tasks and the ministry of God's work—would probably not have a chance to be heard, and there would be concern among these persons that less representation on the floor would mean a decrease in the input of the constituency of the entire Church. They would feel, perhaps, that all viewpoints were not being heard.

The length of time required for the conduct of Convention business is also of concern for some people within the Church.

At present, thirteen days are required for the entire agenda—ten legislative days plus three additional ones. One and a half days are given over to rest and relaxation at midpoint between the two weeks. It is believed that these are necessary for the release of tensions that build up during the hectic schedule of the first week. Whichever view prevails at this point, it is becoming increasingly apparent that much is to be gained by a shorter Convention period.

There are some members of the Church who cannot afford to be away from their professions or employment for this period of time; and there are family responsibilities, especially in the case of younger women, which precludes their presence and participation in an overlong Convention. Along with this consideration is the direct relationship between the length of Convention and the cost. Many feel that the rising costs could be reduced by shortening the period of meeting. In fact, eliminating only one day of General Convention would result in costs going down dramatically.

Over the years, the geographical location of the meeting of General Convention has gravitated from the Northeast to the center of the United States. The last Convention held in the population center of the Church was in Boston in 1952. Out of the sixty-five General Conventions, only nineteen have met in the Midwest and Far West. A study of the dioceses and the numbers of deputies from each diocese attending General Convention indicates a gravitation to meeting in the center of the United States. Ideally, from the standpoint of travel convenience, General Convention should be held in the triangle formed by Chicago, Louisville, and Pittsburgh. Because of the physical needs of the convention facility, the numbers of hotel rooms required, and the costs involved, there is no possibility at present of General Convention meeting in larger cities within this triangle. However, it is meeting in larger cities in the center of the United States having adequate convention facilities and enough hotel rooms reasonably priced and convenient to the convention facility itself. This is also an equitable arrangement for the transport of deputations, since it does not require the movement of large numbers of persons from one coast to another.

There has been a proposal that General Convention meet on a rotating basis between the East Coast, the Midwest, the West Coast, back to the Midwest, and concluding the rotation on the East Coast. This plan has been studied by the General Convention Manager and found not to be feasible at present due to the special requirements and logistics of General Convention. It is generally more economical to meet away from the large population centers on either coast and travel only to the center of the country from each coast.

The time of year in which General Convention has been traditionally held has come under question in recent years. Some have felt that meeting in September and October eliminates some persons within the Church, particularly the school-age youth. As schools usually open their sessions in early September, young people desiring to attend General Convention would be absent for two weeks. Thus, it has been suggested that Convention be moved to August. However, this is the traditional month for vacations throughout the Church, and the idea has not been met with too much enthusiasm. The shores and the mountains have a strong hold upon many Episcopalians. And, of course, there must be a time for busy people to rest and relax. July would be the next alternative, but that is also a vacation month and is the month just between the close of schools and the month when many must begin to think about schools opening in the fall. So July is also not very attractive to many. In June some schools are still in session, and May is too early for others. When this subject is analyzed closely, there is no ideal time for General Convention to meet. Therefore, September or October have become, through tradition, the best possible months for the meeting of General Convention.

The South Bend Convention in 1969, meeting on the campus of Notre Dame University, still remains a memorable experience to those who attended. It was a new style of Convention, called for a special purpose, and one that many throughout the Church would like to have repeated. The Notre Dame campus created a sense of community for that Convention. Through dormitory housing and cafeteria meals, many meaningful interpersonal relationships were created. It was this community feeling that proved helpful in the confrontation of the issues left uncompleted from the 1967 General Convention in Seattle. On the other hand, there were those who chose not to stay in dormitory housing, preferring to stay in motels off campus and to commute to each day's proceedings. The desire to return to this style of Convention is still expressed, and some effort is exerted from time to time to cause General Convention to select a campus setting.

This idea has been complicated by several factors, one being that most universities of the size needed for General Convention have summer sessions and students who remain in dormitory housing throughout the year. August is the only month available to the maintenance departments for the cleanup, custodial care, and renovation necessary before the start of the fall session in September. Again, if a university could contain General Convention, it would have to be for a longer time than the six-day period at South Bend. Additionally, campuses do not usually lend themselves to the tightly knit, compact facilities of a convention hall having self-contained meeting rooms for all functions. Long distances between committee meeting rooms and both Houses would, of necessity, lengthen the time required for the agenda.

Another factor concerning a campus Convention would be that the wear of thousands of daily footsteps upon the playing service of the gymnasium floor would not be acceptable to the athletic department. So, even though there is great sentimentality built up in the afterglow of South Bend, there is a certain impracticality in having that arrangement for a full Convention today.

These are some of the continuing and constant discussions surrounding the General Conventions of the future. Any attempt to predict what can or will happen would be imprudent. We will, therefore, turn our attention to other areas which could affect the future of General Convention. One area could be the matter of its organization.

The actual organization of General Convention seems to be intact in its present form—a bicameral legislative body. The Executive Office of General Convention with its particular function, described in the previous chapter, together with the function of the Executive Council, described in chapter 5, appears to be fairly well delineated. It has been felt by some that the incorporation of the Executive Office of General Convention into the Executive Council would be a move toward greater efficiency and coordination. On the other hand, there are those who oppose such an idea, for they believe this would violate the intent of the Constitution which establishes the distinct role of each and how they shall operate in concert with one another. These two offices and their staffs operate in entirely different areas and are concerned with totally different objectives.

The issues before the General Convention in the mid-1970s are still focused upon persons and social problems. There was the period of missionary expansion in which the Church was reaching out to the people and problems of other lands. As the Church grew within an overseas area and its episcopate became established, this soon had its impact on the meetings of General Convention. The missionary overseas dioceses received seats for their bishops in the House of Bishops and for their deputies in the House of Deputies. The education and training of native persons in the faith of our Lord within the Episcopal Church soon made it possible to have native-born bishops consecrated, replacing the bishops sent from the United States to establish the Church in each of the overseas countries. In recent years the trend has been to bring American-born bishops and clergy back to America and have native priests and bishops serve in their places. This development has created a truly international aspect at General Convention, and it is now common to have over 150 persons from overseas serving in both Houses.

Another important area for concern for the future of General Convention is that of the youth of the Church. As every generation of young people appears to be quite different from every other, finding different solutions and having different goals and values, it seemed necessary to develop a program that would try to meet these changing needs on a continuing basis. This resulted in the establishment in 1970 of the General Convention Youth Program, which attempts to identify areas of concern and ministry for and to the young people of the Church. As a result young persons have become increasingly visible at General Convention. Sometimes schools and churches provide transportation for these young Episcopalians, and sometimes, just to be present at Convention, they hitchhike long distances with little or no money. Special sleeping and eating arrangements are usually made for them and places of recreation provided. Some groups have banded together in what has been called an "underground coalition" to try to effect changes or to draw attention to some of their various causes and concerns by singing, marching, or demonstrating. Youth and youth advocates have become an effective presence at General Convention, and it is hoped that their interest and participation will continue and will always be a vital part of Conventions of the future.

General Convention has confronted Prayer Book revision twice and, at the present time, is facing the issue again. It has become a divisive issue in some dioceses and parishes and much emotion has become centered upon it. The General Convention is the arena for its full and complete debate. The "1970 Services for Trial Use," commonly referred to as the "Green Book," because of its color, was authorized at Houston; and the "1973 Services for Trial Use," known as the "Zebra Book" because of the stripes in its cover design, were replaced by yet a third edition of trial services prior to the Minnesota General Convention in 1976. Known as "The Draft Proposed Book of Common Prayer," it became the final form of revision prepared by the Standing Liturgical Commission for presentation to the Convention. Acceptance of the proposed revision and its final vote will be given at the Colorado General Convention meeting in Denver in 1979.

One of the most volatile issues the General Convention has ever had before it is the subject of the ordination of women to the priesthood. This has also been the subject for debate in other communions, such as the Roman Catholic Church, the Methodist Church, and the Presbyterian Church. Because of the furor and debate going on throughout the Church, a special meeting of the House of Bishops was called by the Presiding Bishop in August 1974. The matter had been debated in the House at the previous General Convention in Louisville in 1973 and at the House of Bishops meeting in New Orleans and it seemed then that there was a favorable reaction on the part of the bishops. The subject was debated again at the House of Bishops meeting at Portland, Maine, in September 1975.

As issues are generally people-centered, they are easily identifiable, but a solution is often difficult because of predisposition and prejudice. One of the issues continually facing the Church is race relations. Blacks, chicanos, and native Americans are seeking equality with their fellow man through General Convention. At present, the American Indian's long and deep feeling of injustice, is emerging and they are seeking solutions. Broken treaties with the white man, fratricide, and abuse are crimes laid at the door of the General Convention and crying out for help. Even through the National Committee on Indian Work created by General Convention and administered by Executive Council, these concerns are constantly before Convention. Pressure is brought to bear through caucuses and lobby groups. This will continue to occur as long as there are persons who are oppressed and who seek justice within the system.

The issue of human sexuality is also an area of concern, which, due to its sensitiveness, has often eluded the free and open debate of General Convention. It is currently before the population of the nation through various media and is therefore of concern to many within the Church. Persons who are confronted with the subject within families, as well as persons who are themselves involved, feel that definitiveness and understanding of the issue are of vital importance. Thus, they turn to the General Convention for help and guidance.

Other issues are not so easily identifiable but, generally, if one is aware of current issues being reported in the various news media, one can have a good understanding of the issues that might be presented at the next General Convention. Amnesty, crime, abortion, penal reform, drug abuse, gun control—these are just a few of the full range of subjects that could come before the General Convention. Only as each session is conducted and concluded will the outcome of each become known. The Church expresses an official opinion in these matters only after full debate and vote upon each of them.

Because of the distinct nature of General Convention, there is what can be termed a "ministry" of General Convention. This ministry is linked to the process of General Convention. It is an obvious ministry and yet a subtle one, which has to be seen as existing at several levels simultaneously. The first is the broadest and most obvious—the ministry of General Convention to the world. A study of the budgets approved at each General Convention reveals a concern for the evangelistic outreach of the Episcopal Church. There is a universal claim laid upon the world by Jesus Christ. The obedience to this claim by the Church has been expressed historically through the domestic and overseas missions. Overseas mission, as well as domestic missions have received appropriations for the selection, education, preparation, supervision, care, and support of both clerical and lay mission personnel. The Committee on Program and Budget provides the vehicle through which new interests and concerns of Episcopalians can be expressed. The new mission fields are first opened at General Convention with the presentation of the vision and challenge made to General Convention by that committee. After the funds have been voted, the program is established through Executive Council, and then the personnel can be enlisted, trained, and sent, in the Lord's name, to the far and near reaches of this planet for the glorious task of laying our Lord's eternal claim upon peoples and nations.

The next level of the ministry of General Convention is in the event itself. The fact that there is actually a gathering of the Church from among 113 dioceses throughout the world is ministry. The Episcopal Church could become static and self-centered if allowed to see and hear only the problems of a certain diocese or community. This would lend itself to parochialism and would serve no lasting value. By having the gathering of the complete Church in General Convention through the election of deputations and the presence of the Church's bishops, the Episcopal Church is framed in its proper perspective. The privilege and responsibility that is given those participants changes their perspective on the Church. Their views, outlook, friends, and understanding of the Church are all enlarged. To be present under one roof where persons of all backgrounds, colors, life styles, and dress become one in the Church is to feel a oneness with God through Jesus Christ. It is stimulating and dramatic—an experience one never forgets.

The opening worship service, where the pageantry and ceremony of the processional contains all the colors of the spectrum in vestments and in native costumes from other lands, tribes, and peoples, is breathtaking. Banners and decorations help highlight the drama of the experience. Just to walk among the people in various native dress and speaking many languages makes one realize that the event itself transcends the person, and one feels part of an event much larger in scope and dimension—the event of the whole Church. Listening to the debates on the floor of both Houses, one senses the real concerns of persons, that there are problems and cares to be confronted, and that solutions must be found.

Thus, the ministry of General Convention at this level is that of broadening horizons. Through debates, discussions, confrontations, and challenges, old ideas may be exchanged for new with the additional information gained. This fosters inner growth within the person, and it is this growth that becomes the bond among the interpersonal relationships of thousands of Episcopalians at the event that can be termed ministry.

The General Convention also ministers to dioceses and parishes. Persons living in close proximity to the Convention city often ask how they might become involved in General Convention. Not being a bishop or an elected deputy, they are unable to attend Convention in an official capacity, and yet they do not want to be excluded or have the feeling of being left out of the event itself. This is the occasion for the astute rector and vestry to prepare the parish for General Convention. There is much pre-Convention publicity, materials, and news, which are ideal resources for training and educational sessions. To teach a parish or diocese about the history, process, and organization of General Convention, as well as to give them an understanding of its current issues is to have a parish or diocese with a ministry and concern beyond its immediate boundaries. Churches are often so concerned with their own program and their own problems that they become isolated and withdrawn from the Church-at-large. Generally, the parochially centered churches will come out of their isolation to oppose an issue or to raise a great hue and cry of negativism on a matter. Yet they will remain silent and unconcerned about the many noncontroversial but vital aspects of the Church's total ministry. A parish or diocese should prepare itself by enlisting volunteers to serve during the Convention.

Usually, about a thousand volunteers serve as pages, ushers, and exhibit aides, as well as in other areas of need. They have a special purpose at Convention, for without them the Convention process would be greatly hindered. People should be encouraged by their dioceses and parishes to visit the Convention. To sit and hear the floor debates; to participate in open hearings; to visit the exhibit area and see the displays of schools, publishers, manufacturers of church goods, and various causes and programs of the Church, is to gain greater insight and understanding of the vastness of the Church and its ministry. To sit in the Visitor's Gallery of either House and listen to discussions about the Church and the issues before it awaiting decision, and then to continue the discussion within one's own parish and diocese, is to be involved as an informed and aware Episcopalian. This is ministry—to the parish and to the diocese. It is the direct result of the ministry of General Convention.

Finally, there is the future of General Convention. There have been times in the history of the Church when its future appeared bleak and its horizon clouded. The division of the Church into North and South during the Civil War, the vigorous debates over High Church versus Low Church liturgy, and the vigorous feeling surrounding the Civil Rights Movement created talk of schism and permanent separation among the various factions within the Church. Today, there is controversy and debate within the Church over Prayer Book revision and the ordination of women to the priesthood. These matters are highly volatile and emotionally charged. However, if logic, reason, and right spirit prevail as the Church debates these issues, the cohesiveness and oneness of the Church will remain intact. It is important to keep in mind at all times that God, not man, is the head of the Church and that it is his redemptive work which is always the Church's first concern.

General Convention will continue to be the forum where these matters are resolved. Some resolutions will result in affirmative action and others will not, but the fact remains that what is done is believed to be God's will for his Church and his people at that moment in time. General Convention remains the arena of concern for God's work, the place where persons may truly speak their minds about issues and yet not be excluded because of a difference of opinion. Episcopalians have often differed on many issues and there have been times when some have left the communion. The genius of General Convention is that it provides for the free exchange of human ideas that are focused upon heavenly causes. For this reason alone, the future of General Convention is secure.

General Convention may not always be structured and organized as it is today. It may have its ministries focused upon different needs. However, one thing is certain: as long as the Church is doing the important work of redemption and reconciliation, the General Convention will be a vehicle to help accomplish that work. That is the work of the Church—and that is the General Convention.